GATHERING OF THE TRIBE

< RITUAL >

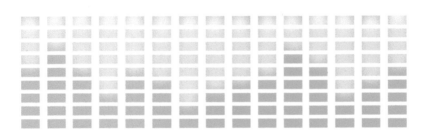

BY MARK GOODALL

HEADPRESS

A HEADPRESS BOOK
First published by Headpress in 2023, Oxford, UK : headoffice@headpress.com

GATHERING OF THE TRIBE: RITUAL
A Companion to Occult Music On Vinyl Vol 3

Text copyright © MARK GOODALL and respective contributors
This volume copyright © HEADPRESS 2023
Cover & layout design: MARK CRITCHELL mark.critchell@gmail.com

The Publisher wishes to thank Jen Wallis.

10 9 8 7 6 5 4 3 2 1

A CIP catalogue record for this book is available from the British Library

ISBN 978-1-915316-21-9 paperback
ISBN 978-1-915316-22-6 ebook

HEADPRESS. POP AND UNPOP CULTURE : HEADPRESS.COM

< C O N T E N T S >

GATHERING OF THE TRIBE

< R I T U A L >

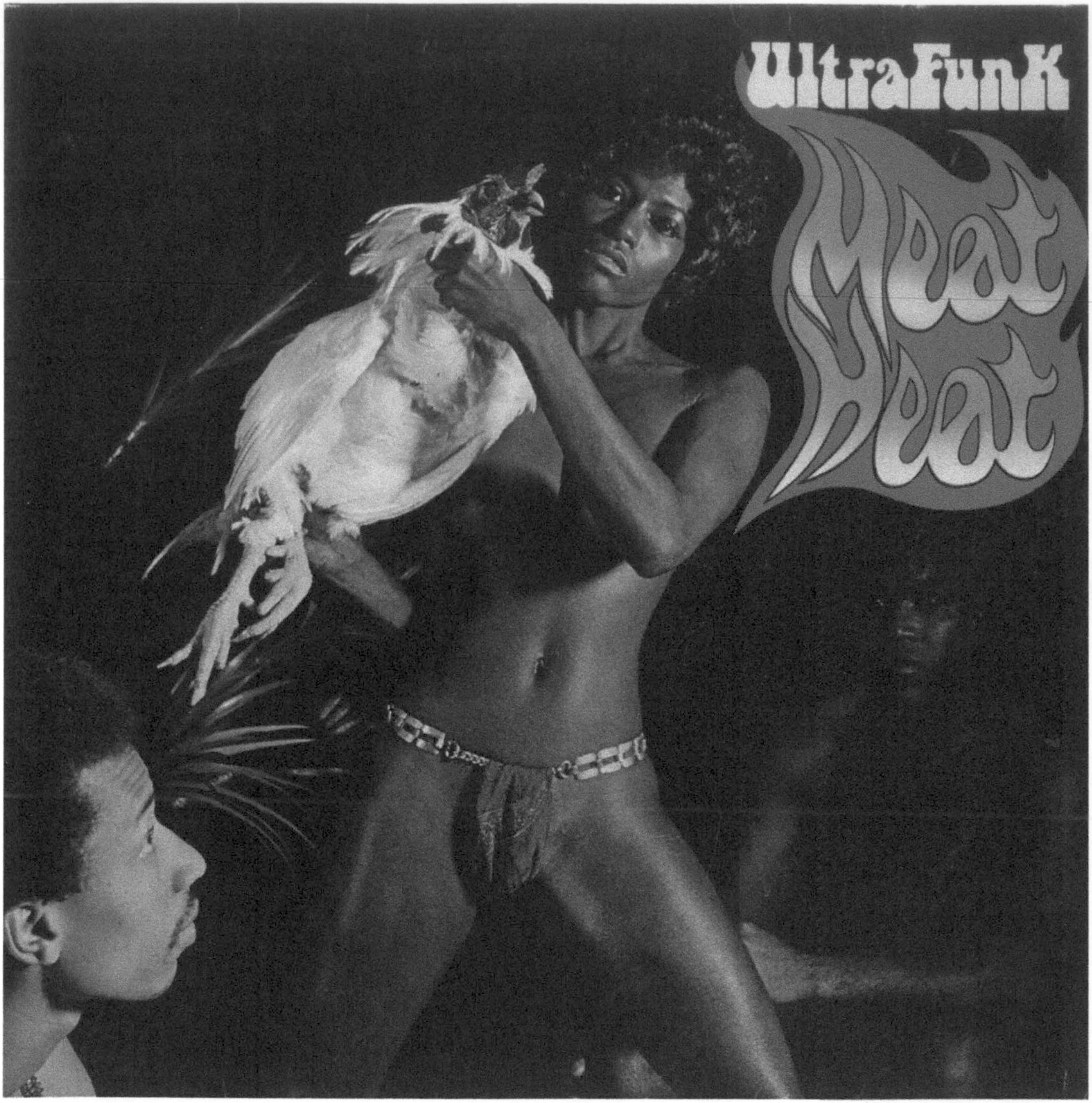
UltraFunK
Meat
Heat

< R I T U A L >

Ritual

"TO THINK ABOUT RITUAL IS TO REFLECT ON HUMAN NATURE, SOCIALITY AND CULTURE".[1]

The writer, musician, and curator Tot Taylor once observed that the word 'ritual' is already present in the word 'spiritual'. That combination of material practice and the transcendent can be found within the strange combination of records discussed in this publication. The physical exertion involved in performing rites or undertaking creative acts can be complemented by the conjuring up of something intangible and weird. This takes place within many human actions, but it is within the realm of sound and music that a particularly fascinating synthesis of sorts takes place. With music, one can transpose imagination, visions, and dreams into 'sacred rites'. 'Heavy conscious creation', the theme of these essays, embodies the realisation of occult and esoteric ideas through artistic expression, in this case the sonic arts. Ritual, according to Taylor, 'helps, heals and inspires'[2]. Composers in the classical realm used sacred folk myths and pagan rituals as inspiration (Debussy, who was discussed in the first volume of *Gathering of the Tribe*, Stravinsky, and — discussed here — Alexander Scriabin), but once popular music expanded into experiments with consciousness, ritual became an integral part of the concept of sound as part of a cosmic whole. Through ritual, music becomes a conduit for the passing on of spirituality, the sound, in Stravinsky's words, a "vessel through which the *Rite* passed".

1 *Ritual*, Barry Stephenson (OUP, 2015), p.1.

2 *Voodoo*, Tot Taylor (Riflemaker 2009), p.37.

< R I T U A L >

The religious and nonreligious ritual records discussed in this publication exemplify the more open aspects of spiritual ceremonies. As James Frazer observed in *The Golden Bough* (1890), his famous and controversial study of customs and belief systems, so-called 'primitive' rituals can be 'performed by anyone and anywhere, as occasion demands' and it is spirits, not gods, that are recognised. In addition, these rites are 'magical rather than propitiatory (trying to please the Gods)' through 'ceremonies believed to influence the course of nature directly through a physical sympathy or resemblance between the rite and the effect which it is the intention of the rite to produce'.[3] The music discussed here is using these elements of ritual to immerse the listener in the experience of a magical rite; it may aid the listener in spiritual enlightenment in some way but may also simply provide entertainment and an engaging listening

experience. Frazer is of course referring to authentic ritual practices, including those treated with suspicion by Enlightenment thinkers, but there are many instances of ritual myths being reworked and perverted for sensationalistic and exploitative means. Haitian Voodoo rituals being sensationalised in popular culture is a good example of this, as well as the use of occult ritual mixed with eroticism for shock purposes (for example, Renato Polselli's 1973 film *Black Magic Rites*, discussed in this volume).

Rites for some can be 'utilitarian, vicious or depraved',[4] but for others can be beautiful and a means of developing a deep and advanced spirituality. Myths are, according to Frazer, 'dramatised in ritual'[5] and that performance of myth through rites that are magical or sacred is the place where music and sound can and does play a key role. The 'religious ritual ceremony', discussed by Antonin Artaud in relation to the Balinese theatre he encountered in 1931, places ritual and the metaphysical at the heart of its expression. The same driver

---

3 *The Golden Bough*, James Frazer (Penguin 1996), p.494
4 *Magic and the Supernatural*, Maurice Bessy (Spring Books 1968), p.33. 5 Frazer, p.730.

< RITUAL >

subsequently found its form in film and music, where sound can cause a direct, concrete effect on audiences lacking in conventional ritualised speech. The creator of the musical ritual becomes 'the organiser of magic, the master of holy ceremonies'.[6] It is possible, through a profound engagement with ritualised sound, to escape from the various notions of 'reality' or attempts at simulating the 'real world', into another realm. After all, art is not 'everyday life' but an extension of it or an escape from its banality. This is why, in many rituals, music and especially rhythm (drums), plays an integral part in accenting and driving the ritual along, releasing the body from the 'normal'. Music integrated into ritual becomes a key dimension of the syncretic process.

The creative arts in western culture became connected to ritual through the idea of 'staging from the angle of magic and enchantment' a 'fiery projection of all the objective rules

6 *The Theatre and its Double*, Antonin Artaud (Calder 1993), p.42.

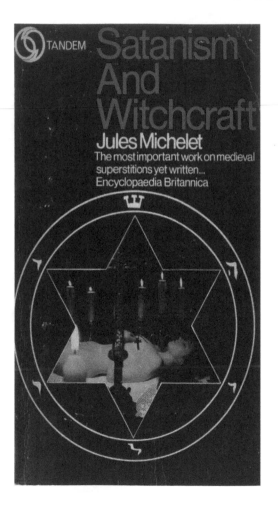

of gestures, words, sound, music or their combinations'.[7] This new theatre would kick life into ritualised performance and put an end to the 'deadly theatre' of the past.[8] Ritual is a form of living action and while records are encountered as objects mostly on the aural plane, an innovative and surprising use of sound can conjure up all manner of images, places, and emotions.

7 Ibid., p.54.

8 *The Empty Space*, Peter Brook (Penguin, 1968).

< BLACK MASS >

Black Mass
LUCIFER (UNI, 1971)

Tracks

> SOLOMON'S RING
> THE RIDE OF AIDA (VOODOO)
> INCUBUS
> BLACK MASS
> THE EVIL EYE
> EXORCISM
> THE PHILOSOPHER'S STONE
> VOICES OF THE DEAD (THE MEDIUM)
> WITCH TRIAL
> ESP

The 'Black Mass' as imagined in commercial exploitation films such as *Witchcraft '70* (1969), *Legend of the Witches* (1970), and *The Satanic Rites of Dracula* (1973) is a sexualised ritual incorporating the Catholic Mass and its inversion, filtered through the Satanic realm. In the Black Mass, symbols are transformed and reimagined, becoming a vivid and lurid tableau incorporating nudity, blood, and sacrifice. Naked young women lie prostrate on an altar while men in robes attend to them in various perverse ways. The Black Mass is a deliberate mocking of and rebellion against Christian beliefs and was popularised in written form long before such films existed, in nineteenth-century books such as *La Sorcière* (*Satanism and Witchcraft*, 1862) by Jules Michelet and *Là-bas* (*Down There*, 1891) by Joris-Karl Huysmans. *Là-bas* contains a description of a torrid Black Mass taking place in a dingy Parisian chapel, so vividly described that it has shaped all subsequent manifestations of the rite, a sensational visual and sexual obsession that captured the modern creative imagination.

STEREO 73111

< BLACK MASS >

In some ways that is how the artist here, 'Lucifer', has developed this electronic version of the Black Mass ritual, taking the core elements and representing its various imagined dimensions in sonic form. In fact, the Black Mass is only one of several occult preoccupations developed on the LP, which also includes highly inventive audio studies of hypnotism, Voodoo, ESP, witchcraft, etc. Unlike the silliness of the populist portrayals in mass media, *Black Mass* offers a sonically powerful articulation of the Satanic ritual.

The 'Lucifer' that made this LP is Canadian composer and Moog pioneer Mort Garson (1924–2008). Garson was a classically trained musician and in addition to writing and producing various pop hits (including 'Our Day Will Come' for Doris Day) and film music, worked in the burgeoning field of academic electronic research. Garson's LPs, *The Connection* (1968) and *Electronic Hair Pieces* (1969), are recognised as classics of supernatural electronic sound. Black Mass is the continuation of that exploration into progressive modulations. Garson's forays into the occult began with *The Zodiac: Cosmic Sounds* (Elektra, 1967), a suite of pieces based on the signs of the Zodiac written by Garson with words by Jacques Wilson (discussed in the first volume of *Gathering of the Tribe*), and concluded in 1975 with *The Unexplained (Electronic Musical Impressions Of The Occult)* under the pseudonym of 'Ataraxia'.

Garson's research for *Black Mass* was serious to the point of incorporating a set of detailed sleeve notes explaining each track by Michael Owen Jones, an American professor of folklore and mythology. Owen Jones 'illuminates' the areas of the occult and witchcraft that Garson has identified for the LP in an entertaining, if exaggerated, fashion.

Black Mass builds atmospherically. 'Solomon's Ring' counterpoints synthesizer oscillations with an exotic sounding melody before a more regular pulse begins, emulating both Solomon's magic carpet and

All selections ASCAP
Published by CAVALCADE MUSIC CORP. / EMANAY MUSIC CO.
Electronic music composed & realized by MORT GARSON
Direction by DAVE WILLIAMS
Electronic engineering by EUGENE HAMBLIN
Produced by PATCHCORD PRODUCTIONS
Jacket design by VIRGINIA CLARK

MCA Records, Inc. 100 Universal City Plaza, Universal City, California and 445 Park Avenue, New York, New York — U.S.A. • MCA Records, Inc. 1971 Printed in U.S.A.

UNI
BACK

< B L A C K M A S S >

his use of a magic ring to conjure up demons. The track ends with a solemn series of slow Moog pulses. 'The Ride of Aida' includes a startling electronically treated voice (akin to the vocoder) that represents the cries of the Voodoo spirits. 'Incubus' introduces a demoniacal sexual element to the LP, the incubus being, according to Owen Jones, a male 'cloven-footed and evil-smelling spirit'. Orgasmic cries pierce the music which then forms into a steady rhythmic beat that is a bizarre metallic bossa nova. 'Black Mass' itself is a majestic sweep of electronic sound. Bells chime as the tension builds with a distorted church organ simulation and high-pitched notes leading to manic arpeggiated patterns and a monolithic beat. A metal gong sound ends the track. 'Evil Eye' briefly depicts the sensation of experiencing a death-inducing stare from a witch, a form of shrieking possession.

Side two begins with 'Exorcism', a series of manic irresistible electronic patterns and improvisations, emulating the violence of the act of cleansing a body possessed by an evil spirit that then ends hopefully in the restoration of a brief but peaceful calm. The alchemist's vision is represented by 'The Philosopher's Stone', a series of deep Moog notes and clanging metal sounds representing the material created in this mysterious form of chemical invention. 'Voices Of The Dead' is the LP's most haunting track, a slow-burning dirge featuring circles of sound swirling around enigmatically. This is the electronic sound of a séance, a conversation across the spirit world with the dead. 'Witch Trial' starts semi-comically with a baroque flourish à la Wendy Carlos before lapsing into a bizarre series of sound bursts. Then the ominous sound of a drum heralds the killing of the witch. 'ESP' is a very short but nevertheless enigmatic finale to Black Mass, a swirling mass of sound representing the transference of matter across the cosmos.

'At last the world of the occult has found a voice in music,' states poet and writer

< R I T U A L >

Jacques Wilson on the sleeve of The Unexplained. Mort Garson certainly was adept at conveying the mysterious sense of the unknown via the modern technology of the synthesizer and tape machine. Although Garson's other 'occult' recordings are perhaps more tuneful and their influence can be clearly discerned in modern-day electronic music (especially the output of labels such as Ghost Box and Castles in Space), Black Mass, representing the effective dark side of the occult in musical form, is far more disturbing and powerful than anything conjured up by the histrionic shenanigans of death metal groups or the pantomime pomp of Satanic rock.

'The Black Mass would seem to be the redemption of Eve from the curse Christianity has placed on her'.[9]

---

9 Jules Michelet, *Satanism and Witchcraft*, p. 82

< WHITE MASS / BLACK MASS >

SONATA "WHITE MASS" (SONATA NO. 7)/"BLACK MASS" (SONATA NO. 9)

ALEXANDER SCRIABIN (CONNOISSEUR SOCIETY, 1970)

Tracks

> SONATA NO. 5 IN F-SHARP MAJOR, OP. 53 (IN ONE MOVEMENT)
> SONATA NO. 7 IN F-SHARP MAJOR, OP. 64, "WHITE MASS" (IN ONE MOVEMENT)
> SONATA NO. 9 IN F MAJOR, OP. 68 "BLACK MASS" (IN ONE MOVEMENT)
> EIGHT ÉTUDES OP. 42 (1903)
> NO. 1 IN D-FLAT MAJOR
> NO. 2 IN F-SHARP MINOR
> NO. 3 IN F-SHARP MAJOR
> NO. 4 IN F-SHARP MAJOR
> NO. 5 IN C-SHARP MINOR
> NO. 6 IN D-FLAT MAJOR
> NO. 7 IN F MINOR
> NO. 8 IN E-FLAT MAJOR

'I HAVE COME TO TELL YOU OF THE SECRET OF LIFE, THE SECRET OF DEATH, THE SECRET OF HEAVEN AND EARTH'.[10]

The Russian composer Alexander Scriabin once wrote that 'there is nothing spiritual which cannot be expressed materially, and nothing material which cannot engender thought'[11]. Scriabin was an intensely spiritual artist, simultaneously expressing orthodox Christian and esoteric beliefs through his music. His symphonic works and operas contain texts that are poetic, romantic, and obscure. Scriabin's notebooks are filled with philosophical ideas

10 Simon Nicholls, *The Notebooks of Alexander Skryabin*, p.67. 11 Ibid., p.60

Connoisseur Society

CS-2032 STEREO

SCRIABIN
Eight Etudes, Opus 42 (first complete recorded performance)
Sonata No. 5
"WHITE MASS," Sonata No. 7
"BLACK MASS," Sonata No. 9
RUTH LAREDO piano

FRONT

< W H I T E   M A S S   /   B L A C K   M A S S >

about the relationship between sound and image and the effect of musical harmony on the cosmic sphere. The creative impulse was a supernatural force; as he saw it 'the world is the result of my activity, of my creation, of my (free) volition'. Cyril Scott described Scriabin as 'the first Russian composer who combined a theoretical knowledge of occultism with the tonal art'.[12] Even his death at the age of 43 from blood poisoning was attributed to his delicate disposition laying him open to 'dark forces'.

Scriabin realised that through music it was possible to summon up new powers, and that the performance of a musical composition was akin to a ritualistic practice. The aim of his piano compositions nicknamed 'White Mass' (1911) and 'Black Mass' (1912) relates to Scriabin's use of sound as a transformative process. This process is mysterious and should be celebrated as such. As he stated in his fascinating but often rambling *Notebooks*, 'I create a black not-I and a white I, and I want to make the not-I white. In this is my free play'.[13] Further, the act of creation can be used against the forces of evil that are summoned

up to be vanquished through the creative act: 'I resurrect you, horrors of the past, all monsters and all frightening, revolting images, and grant you full flourishing'.[14] Scriabin's 1906 symphonic work 'The Poem of Ecstasy' demonstrates his fascination with H.P. Blavatsky and Theosophy. His use of what was called the dissonant 'mystic chord' was subsequently adopted for use in many a horror or thriller score. The 'poem' resembles some of Debussy's symphonic works but Scott claims Scriabin to be 'in touch with a higher state of Deva',[15] and in his music to evoke ecstatic states more powerfully than the French master.

The 'White Mass', supposedly written as an antidote to the nightmarish quality of his sixth piano sonata of the same year, is a piano sonata in one movement that begins like a darker and more crazed version of Schuman's 'Prophet Bird',

---

12 Cyril Scott, *Music; Its Secret Influence Through the Ages*, p.132. 13 Ibid., p.75 14 Ibid., p.81.
15 Scott, p.134. Scott refers to 'Deva Evolution' as a creative force (art, music) evoking higher spiritual dimensions not otherwise accessible to humankind.

ЅⲤRIABIN

Eight Etudes, Opus 42 (first complete recorded performance)

Sonata No. 5 in F Sharp Major, Op. 53

"White Mass", Sonata No. 7 in F Sharp Major, Op. 64

"Black Mass", Sonata No. 9 in F Major, Op. 68

RUTH LAREDO, piano

By thirty most of us have lived only half our lives. In 1903 Scriabin, at thirty-one, had already written half his music—but he had scarcely more than a decade left to live. That year, the year of the Eight Etudes, Opus 42, was a midway point in his creative activity as well as in his career. Janus-faced, he was looking into the future while holding to the past. He was carrying Romanticism to its ultimate point and simultaneously sounding its end . . . or at least directing it into the colder, less human direction that present-day music eventually took.

1903 was also a turning point in Scriabin's personal life. After four years of sitting like an automaton at the Moscow Conservatory—he was the youngest professor ever hired there—he resigned. "I can't bear to hear other people's music all day long and then write my own at night," he complained. He also had decided to abandon Russia. "In Switzerland, land of the free, they will understand my new dreams . . ." His homeland was not all that he wished, or needed, to relinquish. He no longer wished to stay with his wife, Vera, but she refused him a divorce. After all, they had been immutably married in the Greek Orthodox Church, although she herself was a "converted Jewess," as the fashion of the day put it.

Painful as it was for Scriabin to part from his three daughters and his one-year-old son, Lev, he was no family man. Besides, he wanted a new relationship with his recently acquired mistress, Tatyana Schloezer, who believed in his wildest flights of mind (on Lake Geneva he would stand in a boat and preach to fishermen), and ecstatically responded to the new notes that were beginning to sound in his music. To complicate matters further, at this time, Scriabin seduced a teenage student at the Ekaterina Institute (where he taught once a week to eke out his slender income). The scandal of this really forced him out of Moscow. He remained abroad until 1909, returning then as a musical hero and the most talked about composer of the day.

In all, Scriabin wrote twenty-six etudes. The Opus 42 Etudes are much more sophisticated than their famous predecessors, the twelve of Opus 8, although they are, as I suggested earlier, a midway point. The Opus 65 Etudes in ninths, sevenths and fifths, are ultimate Scriabin—in the vein of the late sonatas. The Opus 42 Etudes abound in subtle complexities (which is why they are etudes): wide reaches over the keys, (No. 1 begins on a symmetrical chord of alternating perfect fifths and minor sevenths; compound meters of five against nine, three against five, four against three; crystalline clear melodies and transparent harmonies. The "ideas" expressed here are also surprising; No. 5 is marked "breathlessly"; No. 6, "exaltedly." However, no matter what difficulties they pose for pianists, the Opus 42 Etudes provide nothing but exquisite pleasures for any listener.

Scriabin's later music constantly pulled away from tonality: thirds were stretched into fourths, and the dominant within the octave was replaced by the augmented fourth (the interval that symmetrically and perfectly divides the octave into half). Strangely, the Fifth (Opus 53), Seventh (Opus 64), and Ninth (Opus 68) sonatas—quintessential Scriabin all—reveal a reminiscent loyalty to the triadic principle. Although the sonatas use minor and major thirds as home base, the music itself explores far distant reaches of sound and meaning.

In December, 1907, Scriabin exhausted himself by finishing, finally, his symphony The Poem of Ecstasy, Opus 54. He wrote to a patron: "The Poem of Ecstasy took much of my strength and taxed my patience. So now you are imagining me giving myself over to rest, something I have wanted for so long? No, not at all! Today I have almost finished my Fifth Sonata. It is a big poem for piano and I deem it the best piano composition I have ever written. I do not know by what miracle I accomplished it . . ."

The miracle was, as Scriabin later explained, that he had "seen" the entire sonata as a vision, a reality outside himself, "sur le plan de l'unite." "I am a translator," he said, and went on to tell how the music was a "three-dimensional body...something existing in the astral world." Of course, giving birth to this beauty "from the beyond," and bringing it into our world meant "a terrible coarsening...a loss and impoverishment of the image." It took Scriabin six days to capture the Fifth Sonata on his terrestrial piano, and another three days to write it down. Because of the Sonata's frequent passages of "imperious summoning," Scriabin appended a few lines of a poem of his own composition to The Poem of Ecstasy, expressive of the heliocentric messianism which was beginning to grip him.

"I summon you to life,
Hidden longings!
You, sunken
In the somber depths
Of creative spirit,
You timid embryos
Of Life,
To you bring I
Daring!"

While the presto con allegrezza passages describe the ecstasy and divine joy of him who dares to answer that call to life, and there are explicit sexual overtones in the now ardent, now languid slow sections, the Fifth Sonata is also a play of light in music. The ending is a blaze of high intensity, sheets of vaporous luminosity, blinding and burning.

Scriabin played the Fifth Sonata for the first time in Moscow on February 21, 1909, and backstage afterwards people fell on their knees before him. Two didn't, however. His old counterpoint teacher, Sergei Taneiev, said tersely: "I feel as if I have been beaten with sticks." Rachmaninoff said: "I think you have taken a wrong direction." But both men later studied and played the sonata. Before too long Artur Rubinstein would premier it in London, to wild acclaim.

Scriabin's favorite piece of music was his Seventh Sonata, composed at the end of 1911. He considered it holy, and even marked passages of it "tres pur." He spoke of its harmonies as "beatitudinous," "saintly," and one day in playing it for friends, he said, "here is my 'White Mass.'" At last he felt he had achieved in music a kind of "sainthood," that he had created something stripped of flesh and expressive of pure spirituality. When he played the opening passages for his intimate friends, he spoke

of "clouds of perfumes," and when the dulcet second theme began, he described it: "the face of the sun dispels the clouds . . ." Here voluptuous is "celestial," eroticism is now rendered "incorporeal . . . dematerialized . . ." "This is no longer music . . . but purest mysticism." And he adored the ending, where a thousand bells seem to go wild, summoned into being by a hundred "trumpets of archangels." The vertigo of the prestissimo ending was to Scriabin earth's final dance, the cosmic explosion before the world is blown to atomic dust, disintegrated and scattering into outermost space . . . making room for a new world, a new race of more highly evolved supermen.

There was always a converse to Scriabin's thinking, he spoke of it as "contrast." As he lay agonizing on his deathbed, he called pain a contrast to the bliss he "normally" felt. He thought the artist must be sorcerer as well as saint, and his biographer Leonid Sabaneyev called him at once "a holy man and a wicked wizard." (Interestingly enough, the word "sacer" in Latin means both "sacred" and "accursed.") "We shall serve both dark and light," Scriabin wrote in his final poem, The Prefatory Action, and, indeed, demonism and evil pervaded his music all his life. The Poeme Satanique, Opus 36, written

Alexander Scriabin in the year 1903

at the same time, oddly, as the radiant Etudes, Opus 42, was the first work with this demonic characteristic. The celebrated Ninth Sonata, composed in the spring of 1913, was the last. Its beautiful second theme, which he sometimes in private called "dormant saintliness," is actually marked "sweetness gradually becoming more and more caressing and poisonous." When he played the concluding march of raucous, corrosive ninths (instead of octaves), he would look away from the keyboard and say he saw visions of "walking nightmares . . . Gothic horrors rampageous . . ." One of his friends, Alexei Podgaetsky, carried away by the grotesque, Boschlike effect of the music, once whispered to him "then this must be your 'Black Mass.'" He whispered because 'black masses' were taken very seriously in Russia. Scriabin was delighted with the appellation, and it stuck.

"Consciousness without sensation is empty," Scriabin confided in one of his secret notebooks, and he aimed at every moment of his music to enlarge sensibility, to introduce "the new . . . ever the new," to extend each limit of the senses.

Whether Scriabin's actual ideas are conveyed or not depends upon the individual listener, but his music as music cannot fail to strike a chord of astonishment. Could there be a more beautiful piece of melodic structure than the Etude, Opus 42, No. 4? Can there possibly be more rapturous sonorities than the allegrezza of the Fifth Sonata? Can more stunning or startling music be written than those clamorous bells at the end of the Seventh Sonata? Can form and progression be more intellectually logical and emotionally true than the Ninth Sonata from beginning to end? I, for one, think not.

—FABIAN BOWERS

Author of the new two volume biography of Scriabin—Published by Kodansha International, Ltd.

RUTH LAREDO

This record of three major sonatas of Alexander Scriabin represents American pianist Ruth Laredo's second recording for Connoisseur Society. Her first record, a Ravel recital, followed close on the heels of a spectacularly successful New York recital in which she included Ravel's own transcription of his La Valse.

Another recording by Ruth Laredo on Connoisseur Society

CS 2005—Ravel
Gaspard de la nuit; Valses nobles et sentimentales; La Valse. Ruth Laredo, piano.

One of "THE YEAR'S BEST RECORDINGS"
Saturday Review

"Her Ravel murmurs without losing lineaments . . . La Valse is a personal tour de force."
The New York Times

"She is a superbly accomplished pianist with supremely even fingers, a cool, jadelike sonority, and a natural rhythmic clarity . . ."
High Fidelity

"Ruth Laredo's playing of La Valse is extraordinary in its pianistic command, rhythmic élan, and interpretive imagination."
The Boston Globe

"Literally ravishing performances . . . a tour de force . . . which includes the most poetic and sensitively conceived Gaspard de la nuit on records."
Columbus Dispatch

SIDE 1

Scriabin	
Band 1: **Sonata No. 5 in F Sharp Major, Op. 53** (in one movement)	10.39
Band 2: **"White Mass" Sonata No. 7 in F Sharp Major, Op. 64** (in one movement)	11.24
	Total time: 22:03

SIDE 2

Scriabin	
Band 1: **"Black Mass," Sonata No. 9 in F Major, Op. 68** (in one movement)	7:20
Eight Etudes, Opus 42 (complete)	
Band 2: Etude No. 1 in D Flat Major	1:52
Band 3: Etude No. 2 in F Sharp Major	1:17
Band 4: Etude No. 3 in F Sharp Major	.52
Band 5: Etude No. 4 in F Sharp Major	1:43
Band 6: Etude No. 5 in C Sharp Minor	2:52
Band 7: Etude No. 6 in D Flat Major	1:42
Band 8: Etude No. 7 in F Minor	1:00
Band 9: Etude No. 8 in E Flat Major	2:09
	Total time: 20:47

Producer: E. Alan Silver / Engineer: David B. Jones / Piano: Baldwin SD-10 / Cover Photograph: Ken Goldberg.

< WHITE MASS / BLACK MASS >

the notes sweeping up and down the scale frantically before settling into a more languid form. The 'White Mass' was Scriabin's favourite piece of music, something that he considered a holy 'saintly' work.

Scriabin's 'Black Mass' was composed as a manifestation of evil in sound form, a Hieronymus Bosch painting transfigured into sound. The piece immerses the listener in a strange world of diabolical fears; a synaesthetic (Scriabin was a keen believer in the theory of experiencing music as colours) rendering of sound into dark imagery. The piece is famed for the demands it makes of the player. It begins ominously with a wash of notes, building step by step to a crescendo. The sonata ends with what Faubion Bowers, who wrote the liner notes for this recording, calls 'a nightmare march of Gothic visions, ghosts and distorted horrors'. The LP artwork is also a vivid representation of these two 'musical rituals', the twin pillars of sacred rites, with the performer, pianist Ruth Laredo, an acknowledged specialist in Scriabin's piano works, portrayed on the sleeve, half in conventional monochrome and in negative.

With these two Masses, Scriabin was expressing his ultimate belief that 'art should reconnect with its mystical origins and should unite mankind in a spiritual sense'.[16] Rites can be practices by artists and musicians as much as religious or spiritual figures and their devotees. In fact, the modern artist is the new conjuror of such mystical spirits.

'When my star flares up into flame
And magic light embraces the earth,
Then will my fire be reflected in people's hearts
And the world will understand its vocation'

('DANCE SONG')[17]

---

16 Nicholls, p.5. 17 Ibid., p.59.

19

PERSONA

< P E R S O N A >

PERSONA

SOM (NOT ON LABEL, 1975)

Tracks

> INTRODUÇÃO
> MONTE
> CÉU
> TERRA
> FOGO
> ÁGUA
> VENTO
> LAGO
> TROVÃO

In 1973 multimedia artist Roberto Campadello (1942–2014) conceived 'The Game of Persona' as part of an installation called 'Casa Dourada' ('Golden House') for the infamous twelfth Art Biennale of São Paolo, Brazil. 'Casa Dourada' was a space built of mirrors and designed for what Campadello

called 'Intro-nautical Journeys': collective initiation sessions, meditations, and cosmic dances.

As Isobel Whitelegg has argued, the (largely collective) proposals put forward for the Biennale were politically radical and 'articulate[d] a history of creative resistance to the Brazilian regime'[18] (of militarist President Emílio Garrastazu Médici). Other modernist Latin American art explosions occurred during this period (Mexico's 'Cultural Olympiad', for example). Yet, despite recent reappraisals of

---

18 Isobel Whitelegg, 'How to Talk About Biennials That Don't Exist: Reassembling the Twelfth São Paulo Biennial (1973)', *Tate Papers*, no.34, 2022 , https://www.tate.org.uk/research/tate-papers/34/biennials- that-dont-exist-reassembling-twelfth-sao-paulo-biennial-1973, accessed 27 June 2022.

FICHA TÉCNICA

Disco produzido por
Roberto Campadello e Luis Carlini

Direção musical
Luis Carlini

Técnico de som
Thomaz Mendoza Harrel

Gravado no Estúdio "Mídia" em São Paulo
Dezembro de 1975

Locução
Roberto Campadello

Canto
Carmen Flores

Guitarra
Echo Play Efects
Gaita
Luis Carlini

Violão
Leo Marcucci

Percussão
Franklin Paolillo

Partecipação especial de
Erico M. Muller
Silvana Perez
Osmar Flores
Zeca

Black Sweat Records

BACK

< P E R S O N A >

the Biennale and the fact that its approved themes[19] chimed perfectly with Campadello's philosophy, he and Persona rarely feature in any of the extant historical studies.

This recording, first issued in 1975 as *Persona, The Game Of Mutations*, is a musical occult rite designed to be practised at home. A box contained a 10" record, a mirror, wooden bases, candles, and instructions to play the 'Game': it was intended, through play and experimentation, to 'dissolve' individual personas into one new entity. Candles are used to light the participant's faces in unusual ways and mirrors are provided to help alter perception in an unusual ritualistic experience. According to the instructions, there should be a 'fusion' in the mirror ... in order to 'build, with the correct superposition, a new face'. Campadello considered glass a material with magical and alchemical properties, a 'permeable membrane that filters the real through the unconscious, an access portal with divinatory and therapeutic qualities ... the guardian of daring allegories and symbols'.[20]

The LP cover image, a woman's face merging with that of a cat, reinforces the realm of the occult, recalling a horror film or the psychedelic work of photographer Dunstan Pereira.[21] In the instructions, further suggestions are made about how to combine the music, light, and atmosphere for erotic, artistic (self-portraiture), and psychic ('transmission of thought') means. The *Persona* game can also be utilised to cure fears (of the dark) and to ease dialogue, a therapeutic dimension to the project that extends the scope of Campadello's mystical vision. The 'game' that Campadello introduces to the audience is, he writes, threefold, exploring the psychological, the magical, and the creative. The titles of the cuts on the *Persona* LP all relate to the 'cosmic elemental' and the I Ching (Mountain, Heaven,

19 Communication and Happenings; Behaviour and Gesture; Everyday Surroundings; Sculpture; Cultural Events; Architecture and the Urban City; Introduction of African Elements in Culture; Nourishment. 20 https://www. blacksweatrecords.com/prodotto/persona-som
21 Especially the cover for the pulp horror anthology *And Graves Give up Their Dead* (Corgi, 1964).

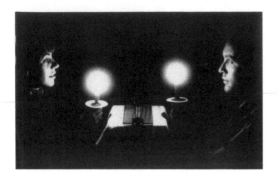

PERSONA BOOKLET

Earth, Water, Lake, Wind), a primary source of inspiration.

The dreamlike and occult sounds on *Persona* can be seen as part of the development of new forms of Brazilian rock, closely linked to the Tropicália movement which was all about blending new elements with previously successful native genres. For the 'Introduction', Campadello initiates the listener into the ritual. His voice is heavily echo-laden. A clock ticks in the background, then more clocks build in intensity. A strange alien music is introduced, weird electronic sounds that have an immediate dream-like effect. After this mysterious opening, 'Terra' comprises a

more recognisable heavier psychedelic rock groove, featuring the duelling virtuosic guitars of Lee Marcucci and Luis Sérgio Carlini (both members of the Brazilian rock group Tutti Frutti which also featured Rita Lee Jones de Carvalho of Os Mutantes). 'Fogo' is driven by tremendously fierce conga drums, revealing the Latin basis for the tracks before more searing electric guitar appears. 'Água' ends side one atmospherically with a haunting echoing female voice (Campadello's wife Carmen Flores) evoking the spirits.

Opening side two, 'Vento', as the title suggests, explores the wind dimension to ritual consciousness. Single bending guitar

< PERSONA >

notes are combined with loud weather sound effects while several objects can be discerned creaking and shifting in the currents of air. 'Lago' is a strange intervention, a more mainstream jam with country music elements such as slide guitar and a straight 'four in the bar' beat. 'Trovão' ('Thunder') is a non-musical soundscape of destruction, an earthquake rumbling ominously towards the listener.

There are two fine unreleased tracks on the reissued version of 2021. 'Sol' ('Sun') is made up of a simple guitar and female vocal expressing the power of the solar orb and could easily be mistaken for a West Coast improvisation. 'Intronáutica' brings Campadello back to conclude proceedings.

Persona is a brief but unique and highly creative exploration of modern psychedelic rock music as ritual. The LP is an indication of the riches to be found in the forgotten or ignored history of Latin American counterculture. The LP was reissued in 2021 by the excellent Italian label Black Sweat, complete with all the elements of

ROBERTO CAMPADELLO

the original package, ensuring that the psych-rock ritual can continue well into the twenty-first century.

Lyrichord Stereo LLST 7341

DIVINE HORSEMEN

THE VOODOO GODS OF HAITI

FRONT

< DIVINE HORSEMEN >

DIVINE HORSEMEN
THE VOODOO GODS OF HAITI (LYRICHORD, 1980)

Tracks

> LEGBA, GOD OF THE SACRED GATE
> DAMBALLAH, SKY GOD (WEDO LELE WEDO)
> AGWE, GODDESS OF SEA CEREMONY
> ERZULIE, GODDESS OF LOVE
> OGOUN, GOD OF POWER
> LITANY (ACTION DE GRACE) AND LIBATION
> GHEDE CHANT
> INVOCATION TO AZACCA, GOD OF
  AGRICULTURE
> AZACCA OSSESSION
> GHEDE, GOD OF CROSSROADS
> AZACCA
> CONGO CULT
> PETRO CULT
> BANDA DANCE FOR GHEDE
> RARA FESTIVAL
> MARDI GRAS CARNIVAL

'IN RITUAL, THE FORM IS THE MEANING'. (MAYA DEREN)[22]

In 1947 the brilliant choreographer, filmmaker, and writer Maya Deren (1917–1961) travelled to Haiti to make a documentary film about the Voodoo religion (Deren spelled it 'Voudon'). The film *Divine Horsemen: The Living Gods of Haiti* took four years to shoot and was completed by Teiji and Cherel Ito in 1977 following Deren's death from a brain hemorrhage. Teiji Ito was a composer and artist who had worked with Deren on her most famous film, *Meshes of the Afternoon* (1943) and created the artwork for this recording (and for Deren's 1953 Elektra LP

22 Maya Deren, *Essential Deren*, p.252.

2 7

ĐIVINE HORSEMEN

THE VOODOO GODS OF HAITI

In 1947 wire recorders (which could operate on automobile battery power) had just come on the market and Maya Deren brought the first one to Haiti. Included in this album are some of the first recordings ever made during religious ceremonies near Croix des Missions and Petionville. These selections serve as a soundtrack to the film she shot there from 1947-1951 documenting Voodoo ceremonies and festivals. As the people walk to outdoor ceremonies we hear the sounds of nature.

Historically, African slaves came to Haiti from various tribes and nations—bringing their particular divinities and rituals, music and dances. They unified their traditions without altogether losing their individual character, into what is called *Voodoo* (Voudoun). The Rada *loa* (dieties), are the protective guardian powers, are the first to be ritually saluted. We hear songs praising Legba, the Guardian of the Sacred Gate to the metaphysical world; Damballah who appears in the shape of a Snake—the positive force which encircles the Universe. When Agwe, Sovereign of the Seas, is invoked we hear sounds of pouring water. A painted raft with offerings of liquor is thrown from a boat and sinks while a haunting song is chanted. Next, Erzulie, Goddess of Love, "Mistress to Man" is celebrated. Powerful drumbeats salute Ogoun, Warrior God of Might and Power. After Ghede, Lord of Death and Keeper of Cemeteries, is invoked, the *Action de Grâce*, prayers in the Catholic form of a litany is heard, and Azacca, the god of Agriculture. In Rada rites 3 baptized drums are pitched at specific intervals and each plays a designated beat to create a distinct song. The high pitched 'petit' drum supplies the energy and holds down an unvaried rhythm. The 'seconde' drum supports the movements of the dancers. The 'mamman' drum with its complex and varied rhythms occasionally contributes a 'break' (cassè) in the beat. This temporary departure sometimes instills a loa in the head of the worshipper (possession). The musical statements are

made by the *drum* and not by the *drummer*. The priest uses an *asson* (a calabash wrapped in a loose web of clay beads and snake vertebrae with a bell attached) to summon the loa. When accelerated, its rattle stimulates the vibration of the ritual. In addition, an *ogan* (bell shaped iron) plays the constant essence of the rhythm.

One hears the music of the Congo Cult who have ceremonies and dances devoted exclusively to Congo traditions. Its roots hold firmly in modern day jazz. There are two drums being played and a third drummer plays on the side of the mamman drum on a board attached to it. It has the feeling of a galloping horse which also incorporates breaks. This is followed by music of the Petro Cult, patrons of aggressive action, punctuated by cracks of whip and whistles. There are two drums beaten by hand instead of the usual sticks. The drumming has a distinctively intense almost nervous off-beat rhythm. During ceremonials the songs are led by a *houngenikon*, and the devotees respond in chorus. The language is Creole of 18th C. French derivation although with African grammatical structure and it contains African and Spanish words. There are moments when the voices of the loa can be heard talking and singing on this recording.

The massive primitive power of these ceremonial drum beats is overwhelming but listen again for the sophisticated poly-rhythms which make up that power; and to the astonishing eloquence of the songs, which ride the beat in a curiously detached way-like a skilled horseman whose body is never bounced by the rhythm of his horse.

The album concludes with the festive mood of RaRa and Mardi Gras Carnivals. The recordings are of bands travelling from house to house playing such instruments as *vaccines*, (bamboo flutes of a single note sometimes tapped with sticks) played in groups of 3 or 4. *Cha chas* (gourd rattles), whistles, trumpets, and Carnival drums are also

used. It is a Springtime celebration of the resurrection of the Life of the Earth. A time of hope and promise of a fresh start and a clean beginning.

Statement of Maya Deren, 1953
"If the songs and drumming achieve the compelling power which I believe to be represented in this album, it is because the microphone, lashed to the centerpost of the ceremonial peristyle, has captured a record of a labor, of the most serious and vital effort which a Haitian makes, for he is addressing himself not to men but to divinity. They are singing for the gods. It is a privilege to have overheard and to have recorded it."

Voodoo as a metaphysical system, its dances, music and rituals are elaborated in the book **DIVINE HORSEMEN: The Living Gods of Haiti (Dell Publishing Co., 1951). Her documentary film on the subject is given the same title (released 1978, Distributor: Cherel Ito, 106 Bedford St. #4e, New York, N.Y. 10014)

Liner notes: CHEREL ITO
Cover design: TEIJI ITO
Acknowledgment: HOUNGAN JOE who initiated Maya Deren into the religion.

ACKNOWLEDGEMENTS:
Houngan Joe, Houngan Isnard Lynch, Houngan Antonio, Pierre (Titon) and Mambo Maya Deren—Great Priestess who are among us now in Spirit.

Also Oddette and Milo Rigaud for their guidance.

< DIVINE HORSEMEN >

Voices of Haiti. At the time of filming *Divine Horsemen* Deren was heavily immersed in the practice of ritual and in considering how, in religious ritual (as in dance and cinema), the human form is not the source of the dramatic action but becomes 'a somewhat depersonalised element in a dramatic whole'.[23] Deren was another westerner fascinated by the myth and violence of Voodoo ritual and knew that secret knowledge was contained within the practices conducted.

Inspired by American anthropologist/dancer/choreographer Katherine Dunham, the initial idea was for Deren to source material to adapt Haitian ritual into forms of modern dance, but the rapture of the experience, in the words of Joseph Campbell, 'transported her beyond the bounds of any art she had ever known'. Deren's 1953 study *The Voodoo Gods* remains one of the most fascinating studies of the religion, being both honest and experimental.

Divine Horsemen: The Voodoo Gods of Haiti is essentially a field recording made during the collection of images for *Divine Horsemen: The Living Gods of Haiti*. Using a wire recorder tied to a central post, Deren captured in detail the actual sounds of the Voodoo ritual as it took place, a clear record of the 'singing for the gods'. The LP reinforces through audio the well-established connections between the rhythms of African religious ritual practices and contemporary forms of popular music (jazz, blues, funk, etc.). This occurs at the level of sound (drums, chants) and thematic content (the myth of the 'crossroads' and transfiguration through movement and dance). *The Divine Horsemen* film captures a variety of aspects of Haitian Voodoo ritual and as a work of the avant-garde does not shy away from adopting techniques that would be considered 'alienating' by more conventional anthropological/ethnographic filmmakers, including freeze-frames and slow-motion effects. Unlike Deren's excellent other films, most notably *Ritual in Transfigured Time* (1946), the 'choreography' here is natural

---

23 Ibid, p.58.

< R I T U A L >

and not as staged or theatrical (although still obviously constructed). There are visual representations (probably deliberate) linking ancient ritual with the modern world. At one point the participants seem to move as one body, a single entity, as at a modern festival. There is also a brief sequence where a woman gyrates with a wooden shaft, a clear precursor to the sexy pole dance of modern nightclub entertainment. This record, like the film, captures the core elements of Voodoo: spirit, possession, and sacrifice.

The most powerful element of the LP is of course the sound of the drums that, after a brief opening section of dialogue and ambient sound, power hypnotically through almost the entire duration of the recording. From the arrival of the spirits at the sacred gate, through the various libations and dances of love, to the brutal sacrifice of animals, the drums never let up. The relentless rhythm is likened to the movement of a galloping horse. Drums are what Deren calls 'the sacred oratory' and are interspersed with chants (the 'call and response' at the core of African music) and blasts of iron percussion instruments and bamboo flutes. Drum patterns can be improvised not, as in jazz, for musical pleasure but are here linked to a vast ritual structure,

With their origin in the Congo region of central Africa, the drums lie at the heart of ritual, their invocatory power aiding the possession of devotees by the living gods. In Voodoo, dance invites possession and the drum 'calls the spirits to be present'.[24] As explained in Cherel Ito's sleeve notes, different drums serve distinct purposes and actions: there are high-pitched drums (the 'petit') that hold the rhythm; 'seconde' drums that support the dance movements, and the 'mamman' drum which is varied and provides what we might today call 'breaks' in the pulse. It is no surprise that Deren's percussion sound recordings have been sampled by dance musicians and producers (Earth, Wind & Fire's 1974 'Rabid Seed' being one famous example of this). The Voodoo sprits are received by the

< DIVINE HORSEMEN >

participants and the music and sound help to facilitate this process.

For Deren, Voodoo conveys the 'spirit of life', the connections between the spirit world and the land and sea. *Divine Horsemen: The Voodoo Gods of Haiti* expresses a true feeling of the evolving and complex forms that Voodoo/Vodou/Voudoun has taken. Despite attempts to mock (as in western commercial films), outlaw, or suppress the religion, it survives as a vibrant spiritual force and, like Deren's extraordinary films, is a carnival of movement, ritual, and sound, the 'only thing of permanence'[25] in an otherwise de-stabilised cosmos.

24 Stephen Grasso, 'Haunted Soundsystem', p.69.
25 *Spirits of Life: Haitian Vodou* (Soul Jazz records, 2005).

ELISABETH WALDO and her concert orchestra

RITES
OF THE
PAGAN

MYSTIC REALM OF THE
ANCIENT AMERICAS

WITH AUTHENTIC
PRE-COLUMBIAN
MUSICAL INSTRUMENTS

Vocalion/Mono VA 8009

< RITES OF THE PAGAN >

RITES OF THE PAGAN
ELISABETH WALDO AND HER CONCERT ORCHESTRA
(VOCALION, 1963)

Tracks

> THE SERPENT AND THE EAGLE
> WITHIN THE TEMPLE OF MACUILLZOCHITI
> CHANT TO THE SUN
> PAPAGANGA LAMENT
> RITUAL OF THE HUMAN SACRIFICE
> QUECHUAN LOVE SONG
> FESTIVAL OF TEXCATLIPOCA
> MOUNTAIN SPIRIT DANCE
> WA-SHO-SHO LULLABY
> PENTITENTE PROCESSION

The western fascination with the idea of 'ritual' is evident in the style of music that became known as 'exotica'. Composer, violinist, and ethnomusicologist Elisabeth Waldo was one of the stars of that genre.

Waldo was born in Tacoma, Washington, in 1918. Her mother was a professional singer and her father a descendant of writer and philosopher Ralph Waldo Emerson. She took up violin aged five and later trained with Leopold Stokowski. After touring as a solo violinist (including in Mexico where she met Diego Rivera) she became fascinated with the soundscape of ancient Meso-American cultures and devised a form of musical 'hieroglyphics' that could translate these pre-Colombian styles into notation that could be rendered on modern instruments.

Her fascination with indigenous musical forms became critical to the artistry of her unique musical style. Speaking of this era she says: 'It was a time when I was most susceptible to the

ELISABETH WALDO

A discovery of Leopold Stokowski, Elisabeth Waldo originally toured Latin-America as a leading violinist in the All-American Youth Orchestra. It provided the inspiration for a unique musical career.

Performer and composer-conductor, Elisabeth Waldo has earned the plaudits of press and public alike; acclaimed "musical archaeologist extraordinary." Her extensive knowledge of Pre-Columbian musical lore is masterfully expressed through her virtuosity as violinist and conductor. Recording Pre-Columbian instruments for the very first time, she rescues the musical values of the Ancient Americas and preserves them permanently for posterity. She unveils the mysteries of a vast North-American Empire, silent for centuries, rediscovering a world of forgotten treasures.

Working with Miss Waldo has been a revelation. Her dedication to detail and her devotion to creating an exact replica of the musical culture of an intriguing chapter of human history qualify her as a musical historian of front rank. She approaches her work with the reverence of an Egyptologist on the continual brink of uncovering one of the lost tombs of the Pharaohs.

Elisabeth Waldo has an important contribution to make in terms of cultural history, in terms of a new world of sounds that originate with her unique instruments and in terms of the sheer pleasure and enjoyment of fascinating music. This is only the first chapter. We will eagerly await an entire series.

GENE NORMAN

"The effect was slightly devastating; the external world was suddenly thrown out of gear, and I found myself sitting in the middle of an upper-Amazon harvest Festival, a veritable riot of tonal color and aboriginal emotion."

DEAN WALLACE, San Francisco Chronicle

COVER ILLUSTRATION: In aboriginal America, priests dressed in the likeness of their Pagan Gods for sacred Ceremonials. The mighty Aztecs believed they saw *Quetalcoatl* re-incarnated when the *Conquistador*, Hernán Cortez, landed on their shores. Thus unwittingly, they aided the Spaniards in their Conquest of Mexico.

We are grateful to the Southwest Museum, Los Angeles, California, and the Stendahl Galleries, Hollywood, California, for their interest and assistance. Engineering Supervision-Rafael Valentin.

Recorded by "Gene Norman Presents", Hollywood.

RITES OF THE PAGAN

SIDE I
1. 3:48   THE SERPENT AND THE EAGLE
2. 3:05   WITHIN THE TEMPLE OF MACUILIZOCHITL
3. 3:00   CHANT TO THE SUN
4. 3:25   PAPAGANGA LAMENT
5. 1:55   RITUAL OF THE HUMAN SACRIFICE

SIDE II
1. 4:15   QUECHUAN LOVE SONG
2. 2:11   FESTIVAL OF TEXCATLIPOCA
3. 2:10   MOUNTAIN SPIRIT DANCE
4. 2:18   WA-SHO- SHO LULLABY
5. 4:00   PENITENTE PROCESSION

All compositions by Elisabeth Waldo

VOGUE RECORDS LIMITED · 113-115 FULHAM ROAD · LONDON SW3 · ENGLAND
Telephone: KNIghtsbridge 4256-7-8

Laminated with 'Clarifoil' made by British Celanese Limited   Printed in England by West Brothers · Printers · Limited, Mitcham

BACK

< R I T E S   O F   T H E   P A G A N   >

"freer" forms of the Hispano and Indigenous Idioms. I became totally immersed in the colour and warmth, the rhythms and mystery of another World.'[26]

Although Waldo issued several recordings based on indigenous South American music, the 'rhythms and mystery of another world' were made most profoundly manifest in her 1963 LP *Rites Of The Pagan*. The expansive range of the 'concert orchestra' learned from Stokowski (who had arranged the spectacular music for Disney's *Fantasia*) is evident on this LP. It is not a capturing of ethnographic sounds 'in the field' issued for commercial purposes, but a reimagining of those ethnic forms for a modern audience fascinated with the mysteries of ancient culture and global travel, as well as a re-working of 'high-fidelity' sounds (another key aspect of the 'exotica' craze). A range of pre-Colombian zoomorphic and effigy form instruments such as flutes, rattles, whistles, and human bone percussion objects feature on the LP, as do some Native American Apache drums.

The LP cover claims that *Rites Of The Pagan* explores the 'mystic realm of the ancient Americas' and in sonic terms this is indeed the effectiveness of the project. 'The Serpent And The Eagle', representing the twin symbols of ancient Mexico, begins with pulsing drums and a cacophony of 'jungle' sounds before Waldo's violin soars above this noise, and perhaps best exemplifies the synthesis of pagan sounds and western classical forms. Sounds come from all around and either assault or immerse the listener, depending on your predilections, creating what Dean Wallace describes on the sleeve as a 'devastating effect'. It ends with a barrage of drums and a soaring wail from which the Eagle emerges triumphant. Waldo describes the music as representing the 'pagan practice of self-sacrifice by blood-letting from ear to tongue' and a struggle between barbaric forces and the Gods.

'Within The Temple Of Macuillzochiti' is more lyrical, dedicated to the natural world

26 https://www.elisabethwaldomusic.com/biography

< R I T U A L >

and the god of music and dance. A staple of exotica — a sensuous high-pitched female voice — carries the principal melody. 'Chant To The Sun' has a catchy, recognisable melody played on the violin, depicting the sun rituals performed at Mayan temples. Other tracks such as 'Papaganga Lament' and 'Quechuan Love Song' also explore the slower, more peaceful, aspect of this musical culture. 'Mountain Spirit Dance' develops slowly, is punctuated by guitar notes and is almost visual in the way it conjures up the atmosphere of a medium designed to 'communicate with the spirits'.

By sharp contrast, 'Ritual Of The Human Sacrifice' expresses how female goddess llamatecuhtli is killed by being thrown across a block before having her heart ripped out with a knife that is then offered to the sun. The musical representation of this is a frenzied round of drums building to a blood-curdling scream worthy of an occult horror film. In 'Penitente Procession' the sound of self-flagellation is simulated and becomes a percussive element in its own right. Strangely, this track also includes highly melodic 'western' orchestral passages, with the effect that the soundscape overall resembles a spaghetti western score. Perhaps this is where Ennio Morricone got his ideas from?

Like all ethnologists, Waldo could be criticised for 'exoticising' ancient American culture. However, there is no denying the vibrancy and immediacy of her interpretation of the mystical ceremonial life of pre-Colombian music and her quest to 'combine primitive and modern instruments in the perfect setting', while demonstrating that this ancient music is as inventive as any modern abstract sound, and just as historically important.

< R I T U A L >

RITUAL

NICO GOMEZ AND HIS AFRO PERCUSSION INC.
(OMEGA INTERNATIONAL, 1971)

Tracks

> CABALLO NEGRO
> NACI PARA BAILAR
> CUBA LIBRE
> SAMBA DE UNA NOTA SO
> BAILA CHIBIQUIBAN
> EL CONDOR PASA
> LUPITA
> PA! PA! PA! PA!
> RITUAL
> ESO ES EL AMOR

A t the semantic level, rituals operate at both ideological and sensory poles of symbolic meaning.[27] Rituals can convey political ideas and relate to concepts to be 'passed down' from one generation to the other, but also to cultural and emotional ideas that are to be 'felt', not simply comprehended. Rituals are physical and emotional.

Unsurprisingly, the complexities of the range of rituals conducted in various parts of the world are not of concern to western creatives wishing to exploit the 'exoticism' of the 'developing world' for artistic and commercial gains. The sexual character (nakedness, performative gesture, symbolism, etc.) of genuine rituals, particularly in Africa, has been commodified and used as a titillating 'hook' for western consumers. The true meaning of rituals (conducted to avert a cosmic or social crisis or to ensure and promote a beneficial

---

27 Victor W. Turner, 'Symbols in African Ritual', Science, 179.

Ritual

nico gomez and his afro percussion inc.

OMEGA STEREO

444.022

INTERNATIONAL

DURECO

FRONT

< RITUAL >

act) and the associated 'ethnographic' images circulating of tribal/ethnic practices have been (mis)interpreted by repressed westerners as 'Dionysian' and 'orgiastic'. In this way connections are made between so-called primitive actions and the actions of the ritual origins of 'first world' artistic expression (especially theatre). As music is an important aspect of many sacred rites it was inevitable that the 'sexy ritual' would also be developed in sound form by unscrupulous, albeit highly creative, individuals.

An excellent example of this is the work of Nico Gomez, particularly his LP *Ritual*, released in 1972 by Dutch label Omega. Nico Gomez is the *nom de plume* of Joseph van het Groenewoud (1925–1992), a Belgian composer and arranger born in Amsterdam. Van het Groenewoud made a specialty of releasing 'exotic' LPs blending Latin/Afro percussion with jazz arrangements, packaged in LP covers featuring semi-naked or naked black women as exotic eye candy (in this instance, a gesturing naked black woman

adorned with colourful markings).[28] Van het Groenewoud was a Dutch deserter from the war in Indonesia who moved to Brussels after World War Two. His father was Dutch and his mother South African. The family emigrated to Curaçao and Cuba, hence some genuine Latin American roots. First training as a violinist, van het Groenewoud made his performing debut in 1946 in a Brussels orchestra as a bass player. In addition to his own recordings, van het Groenewoud worked as an arranger for Belgian pop artists such as Adamo, Claude Michel, and Rita Deneve. His son is the hugely popular Belgian singer and poet Raymond van het Groenewoud.

Emerging at a high point of experimentation with new rhythms and styles and the start of the globalization of 'world music', *Ritual* exemplifies both the gender conservatism and musical radicalism of the scene in that epoch. The LP is a powerful blend of Latin/Afro funk

---

28 Van het Groenewoud also co-founded the Belgian-Cuban group The Chakachas, a collaboration with composer, drummer and painter Gaston Bogaert.

grooves and combines cover versions of Latin favorites (Perez Prado's 'Caballo Negro' and 'Lupita'), a samba/*bossa nova* classic ('Samba De Una Nota So'; Gomez later released an LP devoted to Brazilian sounds), with Gomez originals such as the slinky funk tracks 'Naci Para Bailar', 'Pa! Pa! Pa! Pa!', and 'Cuba Libre' which recalls an early Santana track. The title track itself is a DJ favorite and was heavily sampled by a range of producers including DJ Krush and House outfit Africanism/Liquid People for their track 'The Dragon'. A pedestrian version of (the already pedestrian) 'El Condor Pasa' is the only let down.

The 'Nico Gomez sound' is a skillful blend of Afro-Cuban percussion with prominent use of modern western instruments such as electric bass and organ. Distorted guitars also feature throughout, a nod to commercialism and the contemporary pop market which was then immersed in various Latin fusions. Cuban chants, familiar from the work of Prado, are recreated using backing singers (none of whom are credited). Out of all the European band leaders of the 1970s exploring 'exotic' sounds as part of their *oeuvre* (James Last, Geoff Love, Bert Kaempfert, etc.), Gomez is arguably the most (musically) convincing at incorporating genuinely exciting Afro sounds into his recordings. This was 'funk for the easy-listening masses'.[29]

Despite the persistent and dubious nature of the use of the imaginary primitive ritual as a sexualised way of selling records (reaching an apotheosis with Ultrafunk's 1977 offering *Meat Heat*), *Ritual* is a highly competent and entertaining recording. Sonically, it showcases the best examples of mixing musical genres from different global locations, with the hypnotic, sexual, and trance-like dimensions of certain rites represented in modern orchestral form.

29 Tim O'Brien and Mike Savage, *Naked Vinyl*, p.186

< RITI, MAGIE NERE E SEGRETE ORGE NEL TRECENTO >

RITI, MAGIE NERE E SEGRETE ORGE NEL TRECENTO

GIANFRANCO REVERBERI, GIAN PIERO REVERBERI AND ROMOLO FORLAI (CINEDELIC RECORDS, 2016)

Tracks

> ORGIASTIC RITUAL
> SECRET ORGY I
> BLACK SECRET (PIANO VERSION)
> ISABELLA'S HEART
> PSYCHO TAPE LOOP
> SECRET ORGY II
> BALSORANO'S CASTLE
> SACRIFICE
> SECRET ORGY SUITE
> A FULL COFFIN
> BLACK SECRET
> SECRET ORGY III
> DECAMEROTIC
> THE REINCARNATION
> BLACK SECRET

'THERE IS HARDLY ANY FORM OF VIOLENCE THAT CANNOT BE DESCRIBED IN TERMS OF SACRIFICE')[30]

Lurid tales of ritual sex practices brought back to the west from exotic lands have been the inspiration for all manner of film and music works. Here, the two are combined in a horror film by cult director Renato Polselli with an outstanding soundtrack by one of the many innovative composers from the golden age of Italian exploitation films, Gianfranco Reverberi (who often worked with his brother Gian Piero Reverberi). Polselli was a filmmaker

---

30 Rene Girard, *Violence and the Sacred*, p.1.

FRONT

< R I T I ,   M A G I E   N E R E   E   S E G R E T E   O R G E   N E L   T R E C E N T O >

who was open about using real-world practices for fantastical and sleazy motion pictures, whether that be sensationalising psychiatric reports about human sexuality or adapting ethnographic accounts of so-called primitive rituals.

Riti, Magie Nere E Segrete Orge Nel Trecento (Rites, Black Magic and Secret Orgies of the 14th Century) is a 1971 psychedelic sex ritual horror film of the kind popular in the late 1960s and early 1970s. Polselli's film could be paired with Mario Mercier's *La Papesse/A Woman Possessed* (1975), which also dwells on the partly imagined sadistic/erotic aspect of ritual drawn from the past and brought back through magic to the present day.

Like Hammer's *The Satanic Rites of Dracula* (1973), the film opens with an elongated representation of a sex/death ritual incorporating the sacrifice of a young woman (here decked out in a miniskirt and knee-length leather boots). Her heart is cut out, an offering to the grey and mutilated corpse of the goddess 'Isabella', a woman executed 500 years earlier as a witch who must return from the dead. The film basically cuts between a series of medieval ritual murders and similar atrocities in the present day, with the same characters appearing in scenes of premature burial, ritual killing, vampirism, and assorted forms of sex magic, all designed in some way to reincarnate Isabella.

The complete soundtrack to the film, with additional music by Massimo Catalono and Mauro Chiari, has only recently been released (by Cinedelic) but two tracks from the score were issued as a 7" single when the film was released.[31] The cover art for both utilises the shot of Isabella being burned at the stake, one a still from the film and the other a painterly representation. Reverberi's music is a stirring combination of 'African' percussion, electronic instrumentation and special effects, jazz/funk vibes, and conventional thriller film scoring.

---

31 'Orgiastic Ritual' was also reissued as one side of a split 7-inch single by the Finders Keepers label in 2013.

RITI, MAGIE NERE E SEGRETE ORGE NEL TRECENTO...

Regia:
Renato Polselli

Lato I

1. **Orgiastic Ritual** 3:47 played by South African Combo
2. **Riti, magie nere e segrete orge** (*Secret orgy i*) 4:05
3. **Black Secret** (*Piano version*) 1:32
4. **Riti, magie nere e segrete orge** (*Isabella's heart*) 3:22
5. **Riti, magie nere e segrete orge** (*Psycho tape loop*) 1:05
6. **Riti, magie nere e segrete orge** (*Secret orgy iI*) 2:07
7. **Riti, magie nere e segrete orge** (*Balsorano's castle*) 1:09
8. **Riti, magie nere e segrete orge** (*Sacrifice*) 1:37

Lato II

1. **Riti, magie nere e segrete orge** (*Secret orgy suite*) 9:21
2. **Riti, magie nere e segrete orge** (*A full coffin*) 0:32
3. **Black Secret** (*Synth version*) 1:07
4. **Riti, magie nere e segrete orge** (*Secret orgy III*) 2:06
5. **Riti, magie nere e segrete orge** (*Decamerotic*) 3:21
6. **Riti, magie nere e segrete orge** (*The reincarnation*) 2:21
7. **Black Secret** 2:41 played by South African Combo

Music by Reverberi G., Reverberi G.P. e Forlai R. except:
I1 by Reverberi G., Forlai R., Chiari M., Catalano M.
II8 by Reverberi G., Forlai R., Catalano M.
1971 Reverberi Edizioni Musicali
Graphic: Gianluca Alessandrini Studio
Cover designed: Michele Targonato

Cinedelic RECORDS
CNST 705
EDIZIONE LIMITATA

BACK

< RITI, MAGIE NERE E SEGRETE ORGE NEL TRECENTO >

The 'ritualistic' sound is provided by South African Combo, which, despite the name, was made up of session musicians recording for the obscure Italian label Tickle Edizioni Musicali. For the title sequence the 'witch' Isabella is glimpsed tied to a sacrificial post amidst hypnotic psychedelic light effects whilst Reverbi's 'Orgiastic Ritual', perhaps his most haunting musical contribution, plays; it is driven by a pulsating bass line, single harpsichord chords, and conga percussion, augmented by orgasmic cries dissolving into the moans of a group of possessed initiates. 'Secret Orgy I', perhaps the most psychedelic track, is atmospheric and haunting, using backwards tape chants and modulating female wails. 'Black Secret' is a brief but beautiful romantic solo piano refrain, used, alas, ineptly in the actual film (there is also a synthesizer version). 'Isabella's Heart' begins with an increasing pulsing heartbeat before African percussion is brought in to ramp up the tension of the ritual killing. 'Psycho Tape Loop' is a simple backwards tape loop with a single organ chord held throughout. It also appears in 'Secret Orgy II'. 'Sacrifice' shows that Reverberi could imitate progressive rock dimensions resembling the scores that Pink Floyd recorded around the time of this film's release. 'Decamerotic' is a silly harpsichord/cello composition with New Orleans and ragtime jazz inserts used for attempted comic effect in the film. 'The Reincarnation' is the creepiest track on the LP. The increasing sound wave effect that starts like rain heightens the sense of dread. The final version of 'Black Secret' is very mournful, with a lone trumpet solo rendering the melody.

Polselli once claimed in an interview that the ritual horror in his films was drawn from the symbols of the Catholic faith he was brought up with, describing this form of Christianity as "an invitation to violence". Like most Italian exploitation films, *Riti, Magie Nere E Segrete Orge Nel Trecento* is made from a series of fantastically lit, lurid, and unforgettable scenes with bad acting, inept editing, and an overall discontinuous narrative and structure that makes no sense at all. For once the Italian

< R I T U A L >

censor's judgement that 'the movie consists of a rambling series of sadistic sequences, meant to urge, through extreme cruelty mixed with de-generate eroticism, the lowest sexual instincts' seems accurate.[32]

The film is surrealistic, perverse, and preposterous. However, the music composed for the film is of a high level of skill and imagination, bringing to life the more sadistic aspects of occult ritual and demonstrating again that first-class music can be created for a third-class film.

32 Roberto Curti, *Italian Gothic Horror Films, 1970–1979*, p.104.

< THE FOURTH REICH >

THE FOURTH REICH — THE COMMUNAZIS EXPOSED BY THEIR OWN WORDS: REVOLUTION TODAY IN THE U.S.A.

VARIOUS ARTISTS (GENERAL RECORDS, 1969)

'SACRED WORDS ACT AS AUTONOMOUS PHYSICAL SOURCES OF POWER'.[33]

The concept of the 'Fourth Reich' represents post-war anxiety about the return of Nazi political power in western political, intellectual, and cultural life. Although this fear was based on events with a direct link to actual Nazi ideology, such as the 'swastika wave' (an outbreak of anti-Jewish vandalism that took place in the early 1960s), in the US a twisted form of conservative logic argued that the fascist impulse was to be found in the emergence of the countercultural revolution. Historian Gavriel Rosenfeld calls this a 'universalizing' process whereby Nazi beliefs are extended across a range of other territories, cultures, and events, sometimes bearing little relation to the rise of Adolf Hitler and his ilk.[34]

The Fourth Reich — The Communazis Exposed By Their Own Words: Revolution Today In The U.S.A. was produced and narrated by Sidney O. Fields, a Christian moralist who made a series of 'public information' records 'explaining' the

33 Edward L. Schieffelin, 'Problematizing Performance', p.204. 34 Gavriel David Rosenfeld, *The Fourth Reich: The Specter of Nazism from World War II to the Present* (Cambridge University Press, 2019).

THE COMMUNAZIS EXPOSED
BY THEIR OWN WORDS
REVOLUTION TODAY IN THE U.S.A.

GENERAL RECORDS

THE FOURTH REICH

ABE FRONT

< T H E   F O U R T H   R E I C H   >

problems of post-war American society to an anxious generation of parents and guardians. These included *Victory Over Drugs, Youth In Crisis, and Guideposts For Youth*, the latter of which was released in the same year as *The Fourth Reich*. Fields also directed the 1962 documentary *The Truth About Communism* narrated by Ronald Reagan, which also made links between fascism and communism. Other LPs of Nazi speeches were issued after the war.

The LP collects several speeches made by prominent left-wing leaders and academics but mainly those by Black Power figures including Black Panther chairman and co-founder Bobby Seale, and Marie Walker Johnson, a member of the Bay Area Black Artists Collective. The speeches (with profanities bleeped out) are interspersed with Fields' commentary on what we are hearing. On the LP cover, Fields describes these Black Panther leaders as 'today's stormtroopers', their purpose a 'violent takeover of the U.S.A.' To cement the idea that the likes of the Black Power

movement and Nazi ideology were linked in some way, the LP absurdly kicks off with an archive speech by Hitler himself and concludes with the famous 'power to the people' rallying cry being mixed in with his nonsense words. Links between fascism and the counterculture arguably did exist, for example in the activities of Charles Manson, but these are ignored by this LP which presents the notion that any 'left-wing' activity is dangerous and the practitioners of it 'Communazis'. The cover artwork is a crude collage of political figures. Placards with 'Fight for Socialism' and 'Bring the War Home' jostle with peace signs and swastikas, visually confirming the confusion about the whole enterprise.

The key dramatic dimension to *The Fourth Reich* is the exploitation of ritual as a form of performance, as opposed to its function as a religious or sacred act. 'Performance as ritual' is about exploiting what Edward Schieffelin calls the 'creation of presence',[35] the capability

---

35 Edward L. Schieffelin, 'Problematizing Performance', p.194.

THE F☮URTH REICH
THE COMMUNAZIS EXPOSED
BY THEIR OWN WORDS
REVOLUTION TODAY IN THE U.S.A.

This recording is a condensation of highlights from actual speeches made at the Black Panther Party's National Revolutionary Conference for a United Front Against (so-called) Fascism, Oakland Auditorium, July 18-20, 1969.

Prominent Communist Party, USA, officials were featured on the program along with official representatives of SDS (Students for a (so-called) Democratic Society) and other major revolutionary organizations in America. Black Panther leaders pledged their organization to the vanguard role in the formation of an American National Liberation Front. The similarity of words and actions of today's "storm troopers" with those of the Nazis of the 1930's is brought out, in effect, this recording is a Declaration of War today against our Free Enterprise System by the New and Old Left Revolutionaries as never heard before in one recording—their manifesto for violent takeover of the U.S.A.

HEARD ON THIS ALBUM:

ADOLF HITLER (Infamous dead Nazi leader)
"Within four months we have eliminated 1.2 million."

BOBBY SEALE (Co-founder & Chairman, Black Panther Party)
"We're going to fight Capitalism with some basic Socialistic programs." "We're going to fight Imperialism (the USA) with proletarian internationalism." "We're going to create ... an American Liberation Front."

CAROL THOMAS (Black Panther Party)
"We need Socialism in practice! We need an understanding of Marxist-Leninist principles so that we may put our knowledge into revolutionary practice."

BOBBY BACON (Young Patriots, Chicago)
"And a gun on the side of the revolutionary ... means solidarity and Socialism."

JEFF JONES (Inter-Org. Sec'y, SDS)
"It's the feeling of SDS, the fight that's being waged on the campuses, when it's waged solely on the campuses is a fight that can end up only on the campuses. That's not where we're at, at all." "The struggle that is going to ultimately defeat the United States ... is going to be an international struggle - it's going to be an armed struggle."

ROBERTA ALEXANDER (Black Panther Party)
"And it even goes down to the sexual levels, whether or not the women are supposed to do so and so for the cause of the revolution, etc."

HERBERT APTHEKER (Top official, Communist Party, USA)
"If J. Edgar Hoover condemns something in terms of great severity, then it must be very good indeed. To be attacked by the chief cop of America is a magnificent tribute."

ANDY STAPP (Chairman, American Servicemen's Union)
"And right now, the American Servicemen's Union is building an army within an army, a worker's militia inside the U.S. Army, and along with the Panthers and others we're going to make that revolution." "We have chapters of the American Servicemen's Union on 60 large military installations in the United States and 40 overseas."

CAROL HENRY (Black Panther Party)
"And as Comrade Mao Tse-tung says: 'Fear no sacrifice, summount every difficulty, and win, win, to victory!'"

ORA WILLIAMS (Black Panther Party)
"Chairman Mao says: 'The revolutionary should be more concerned about the party ... than about any individual, be it mother, wife or child!'" "The Red Rock is my bible – the gun is my staff!"

SUSAN KER (ASNE Local, UC, Berkeley)
"You hear all this beautiful revolutionary rhetoric, and see all these 'right ons' out there and raised fists - I think it's great!"

MARLENE DIXON (Doctor of Sociology, UCLA)
"The radical women's liberation movement was created by an international revolutionary movement and is part of it. 'The history of revolutionary struggle is the history of failure, but you only need to win once.' And we shall!"

RAY "MASAI" HEWITT (Minister of Education, Black Panther Party)
"The best defense is a good offense - that's why we dropped that 'Self Defense' ... long time ago. There's no need for it in the name for the Black Panther Party."

WILLIAM KUNSTLER (Communist Front Lawyer)
"It is almost worse to be ready and able to defend yourselves and to freeze on the trigger when the time comes."

DON COX (Black Panther Party)
The Black Panther Party has a motto. We are the advocates of the abolition of war. We do not want war - war can only be abolished through war. In order to get rid of the gun, it is necessary to pick up the gun."

NOEL IGNATIN (Int'l Harvester Worker, UAW, Chicago)
"It is no more possible to bring in a militant rank and file leadership into one of these unions by peaceful, legal means, than it is possible to seize State power by peaceful, legal means."

RON DENNIS (Transport Worker's Union, San Francisco)
"White workers have an obligation to align themselves with the revolutionaries ... to fight a common enemy."

ARCHIE BROWN (Communist Party, USA)
"I think we can help win the working class and their unions to a program to defeat fascism (the USA) for progress and Socialism in this Country."

BOB AVAKIAN (Revolutionary Worker's Union)
"... the proletarian forces like the Black Panther Party, already are taking the lead in forging a United Front which will not only beat back fascism (the USA), but can actually overthrow the imperialist (USA) system."

KENNY HORSTEN (Black Panther Party)
"... the life and death struggle with reformism will begin, it has begun. How this struggle will end will depend upon how completely the masses shake free of the present reformist leadership, and put up militant resistance."

CHARLES GARRY (Revolutionary Lawyer)
"We hope to be able to ... through the National Lawyer's Guild, to be able to have seminars throughout the United States to have lecturers and study courses for lawyers and law students."

This album is presented in the hope that the public will better understand that the present Communazi threat is not a political issue, but a matter of national survival.

Commentary by Sidney O. Fields, the writer, producer and editor of this album. Mr. Fields has written and produced the following documentary films: "Communist Accent on Youth," "Communism & Coexistence," "Communistic Imperialism," (Host and Narrator, Hary Von Zell); "Truth About Communism," Host and Narrator, Ronald Reagan; Currently in production, "Communists on Campus."

United Sales American,
P.O. Box 3636, Hollywood, Calif. 90028.
UNABRIDGED — No. R-2484
ABRIDGED — No. 2485

BACK

of oral communication to create altered states of mind in those taking part in these rituals. The virtuosity of the great public speakers, and the exploitation of the performative dimension as a key aspect of 'being human', is something that both right- and left-wing ideologies have made use of, creating a ritual performance that beguiles and entrances their audiences. *The Fourth Reich*, by using sound recordings of actual speeches, makes this abundantly clear. It is the power of the sonic dimension in ritual — what philosopher J.L Austin calls 'speech acts' — that the LP captures most effectively.

White Christian moralists such as Sidney Field found the words of Black Power leaders terrifying, and rightly so. The defiant revolutionary spirit of the 1960s challenged the status quo, particularly in the US. It was an essential dimension to the counterculture movement, designed to enact permanent change in the ways in which people of colour lived in western societies. While *The Fourth Reich* was designed to frighten righteous bigots into action, it stands as a record of how powerful ritual practices and performance can be in the service of total revolution.

The idea of 'The Fourth Reich' exemplifies the fear of something that so far has not yet happened. The performance rituals captured on this bizarre recording, rather than repulsing the listener, exist as aural records of real and existing change emerging as a positive force in the modern world, the complete opposite of fascism.

'This album is presented in the hope that the public will better understand that the present Communazi threat is not a political issue, but a matter of national survival'. (From the sleeve notes to the LP)

FRONT

< A GENUINE TONG FUNERAL >

A GENUINE TONG FUNERAL
THE GARY BURTON QUARTET WITH ORCHESTRA (RCA 1968)

Tracks

> THE OPENING; INTERLUDE (SHOVELS);
  THE SURVIVORS; GRAVE TRAIN
> DEATH ROLLS
> MORNING — PART ONE
> INTERLUDE: "LAMENT"; INTERMISSION
  MUSIC
> SILENT SPRING
> FANFARE; MOTHER OF THE DEAD MAN
> SOME DIRGE
> MORNING — PART TWO
> THE NEW FUNERAL MARCH
> THE NEW NATIONAL ANTHEM; THE
  SURVIVORS

Produced by an all-star cast of musicians including leader and vibraphone player Gary Burton, Carla Bley (piano), and Burton regulars Steve Swallow (bass), Larry Coryell (guitar), and Steve Lacy and Leandro 'Gato' Barbieri on saxophones, this 'dramatic musical production based on emotions towards death' is a ritual in sound. Although credited to Burton and his quartet, the music was composed and directed by Bley as a 'suite' and was sadly ignored on its initial release in 1968 (submerged by the 'overwhelming tide of free jazz', according to critic Lauren Goddet in the sleeve notes). Bley's skill in combining the aesthetic of Brecht music hall plays with 'one of Mingus's zanier outings'[36] are given full force here and are typical of Burton's then fascination with synthesising different modern musical genres.

The Chinese 'funeral' that is the basis for the recording was held in Hong Kong and spotted by Bley on US TV as part of a French

36 Charles Fox, *The Jazz Scene*, p.30.

RCA
MASTERS

PL 42766
STEREO
DE LUXE
RC 240

The Opening
Interlude: Shovels
The Survivors
Grave Train
Death Rolls
Morning—(Part one)
Interlude: Lament
Intermission Music
Silent Spring
Fanfare
Mother of the Dead Man
Some Dirge
Morning—(Part Two)
The New Funeral March
The New National Anthem
The Survivors

RCA éditeur

1, AVENUE MATIGNON - 75008 PARIS
marque et décision (?) Registered trademarks of
used by authority and under control of RCA Corpo-
ration Made in France from master recordings
owned et controlled by MCA Records.

Gary Burton («vibraphon»); Larry Coryell (guitare); Steve Swallow (basse); Lonesome Dragon (batterie)
plus Steve Lacy (saxo soprano); Mike Mantler (trompette); Leandro "Gato" Barbieri (saxo tenor); Jimmy
Knepper (trombone et trombone basse); Howard Johnson (tuba, saxe baryton); Carley Bley (piano, orgue,
chef d'orchestre).

Juillet 67

BACK

< A GENUINE TONG FUNERAL >

documentary film. That said, it is hard to link any specific and authentic practice to the record as it is more a collection of pieces evoking the ending of life and the subsequent transcendence to another realm.

'The Opening' is appropriately funereal in tone, conveying the unfolding of a solemn ritual in action. 'Interlude (Shovels)' seems to represent, with stabs of brass and tinkling vibes, earth being tipped into a grave. The first appearance of 'The Survivors' is a somewhat comic representation of mourners filing past the coffin and exchanging stiff greetings. Despite the subject matter, black humour is evidenced by some of the titles ('Grave Train' for example and 'Death Rolls', a mini discordant drum solo); Bley herself described the mood as 'irreverent'. Conventional musical elements (a brisk military phrase; listless New Orleans funeral music) are mixed with more abstract sounds so that the general feeling is one of a highly 'visual' event unfolding in front of the listener. The strange conflicting moods of a death ritual are evoked in sound: 'Fanfare' is ominous while 'Morning' and 'Interlude: "Lament"' are lyrical and reflective. The final standout track on side one, 'Silent Spring', showcases the talents of Barbieri. The guitar and bass perform a brief duet before giving way to a relentless baritone pulse and wailing tenor saxophone, set off by Burton's magical vibraphone, which brilliantly expresses the dread and anguish of loss. After a brief pause the instruments combine to develop an East Asian-flavoured coda.

On side two, the incredible, almost static, 'Mother Of The Dead Man', issued previously in a longer version on Burton's second LP *Lofty Fake Anagram*, manages to inject some slinky sexiness into the affair, suggesting that the mourner in question is young and attractive. 'Some Dirge' picks up the tradition of the Latin lament expressing mourning or grief and is complex, dramatic, and at times Felliniesque. The screaming cacophony of 'The New National Anthem; The Survivors' expresses the chaos and despair of death and its associated rituals. This second iteration of 'The Survivors'

GARY BURTON QUARTET

Poet Philip Larkin was normally averse to experimental forms of jazz and described *A Genuine Tong Funeral* in his *Daily Telegraph* review as a 'bit of nonsense'.[38] However, David Sterritt in *Downbeat* described *A Genuine Tong Funeral* as 'sardonic and deeply moving'.[39] Burton has always tended towards mysticism and abstraction in his work but with an ear for more accessible, even humorous, representations of musical ideas. In a short space of time *A Genuine Tong Funeral* conveys all sides of this quest for truth through the medium of jazz. Like all revolutionary works, *A Genuine Tong Funeral* was ahead of its time and instigated, for better or worse, other jazz concept LPs such as Charlie Haden's 1971 *Liberation Orchestra* and other Carla Bley projects.

is reprised for those left in the land of the living but are scarred by the morbid hand of death.

A Genuine Tong Funeral is a mysterious piece of music, with a distinct 'brooding processional quality'.[37] It was bizarrely performed live in 1969 on the US TV show *Mixed Bag*, the musicians appearing in monks robes for the sombre parts of the suite before changing into more light-hearted costumes (cowboy hats, pyjamas, parkas) for other sections. This performance confirms the deeply performative aspect of the piece and how it was conceived as a ritual in sound to be physically enacted.

Genuine or not, music can only postpone the inevitable: death waits for us all.

37 Richard Cook and Brian Morton, *The Penguin Guide to Jazz on CD*, p.225. 38 Philip Larkin, *All What Jazz*, p.236. 39 *Downbeat*, May 15 1969, p.23.

< DISQUE ROSICRUCIEN >

DISQUE ROSICRUCIEN
ORDRE ROSICRUCIEN A.M.O.R.C.
(EDITIONS ROSICRUCIENNES)

Tracks

> INVOCATION POUR SANCTUM
  (INVOCATION FOR SANCTUM)
> CONTACT AVEC LE SANCTUM CELESTE
  (CONTACT WITH THE CELESTIAL
  SANCTUM)
> EXERCICE SUR LES SONS DE VOYELLES
  (EXERCISES IN VOWEL SOUNDS)
> RESPIRATION AVEC SONS DE VOYELLES
  (BREATHING WITH VOWEL SOUNDS)

Rosicrucianism is a mysterious spiritual and cultural movement that developed in the early 17th century based on the mystical knowledge of Christian Rosenkreuz (who may or not have existed). *The Chymical Wedding of Christian Rosenkreutz* is a 'strange alchemical romance'[40] inspired by *Monas Hieroglyphica*, written by alchemist John Dee in 1564 and published in Strasbourg in 1616, often described as the third of the Rosicrucian manifestos (the other two being the *Fama* and the *Confessio*). *Chymical Wedding* later inspired a terrible LP by Iron Maiden's Bruce Dickinson while Dee's work was adapted into an overrated opera LP by ex-Blur singer Damon Albarn.

The Rosicrucians are an esoteric order devoted to the doctrine of building esoteric truths of the ancient past, combining practices of alchemy, hermeticism, and Christian mysticism with elements drawn from the Kabbalah as well as those from 'scientific' areas as diverse as physics, metaphysics,

---

40 Frances A. Yates, *The Rosicrucian Enlightenment*, p.30.

DISQUE ROSICRUCIEN

Symbole dessiné par le Dr H. Spencer Lewis

(Ce symbole, tel qu'il est utilisé ici,
n'a aucune signification sectaire ou religieuse.)

< DISQUE ROSICRUCIEN >

biology, psychology, parapsychology, comparative religion, traditional healing techniques, health, intuition, ESP, meditation, sacred architecture, symbolism, and that mystical state of consciousness relating to the experience of unity with the Divine.

Music has always played a significant role in Rosicrucian practices. For Rosicrucians music is key to the notion of a 'universal harmony' and many early illustrations of cabalist-alchemist workshops incorporate musical instruments (lutes, violas) in their design. French composer Erik Satie composed his 'Sonneries de la Rose + Croix' in 1891 and 'Le Fils des Etoiles' in 1892, having become a member of the French version of the group set up by Joseph Péladan, High-Priest or 'Sâr' of the 'Rose + Croix du Temple et du Graal', to give it its full title. Péladan ordained Satie as 'official composer' of the 'Rose + Croix'. Rollo Myers describes Satie's music here as 'mystical and ritualistic', thus adhering to the principles of the ancient myths. After his spilt with Péladan, Satie

continued to compose quasi-religious and ritualistic forms of music.

There have been several incarnations of Rosicrucianism, and the recording discussed here, while in French, was produced by the American manifestation called The Ancient and Mystical Order Rosae Crucis (AMORC) instigated by Harvey Spencer Lewis in 1915 (he also became its first Imperator). Lewis was initiated into the Rosicrucian Order in 1909 in Toulouse. AMORC's teachings draw upon ideas of the major philosophers, particularly Pythagoras, Thales, Solon, Heraclitus, and Democritus but used the technology of recorded sound to promote their activities. Several AMORC discs exist, including a flexi disc of ancient Vedic mantras (the 'mystical

**EDITIONS
ROSICRUCIENNES**

56 , Rue Gambetta
. 94 190 .
Villeneuve _ Saint _ Georges

Face   A

Face   B

INVOCATION POUR SANCTUM

EXERCICES   SUR   LES   SONS

DE VOYELLES

CONTACT AVEC LE SANCTUM

CELESTE

RESPIRATION AVEC SONS

DE   VOYELLES

par le Dr. H. Spencer Lewis

adapté en Français et enregistré par Raymond Bernard

BACK

< DISQUE ROSICRUCIEN >

intonations of the ancients', the sleeve states) and a 10" record of slightly sinister instructions for children, The Seeds Of Truth Must Be Planted Early.

Disque Rosicrucien is a set of instructions explaining Rosicrucian beliefs based on Harvey Spencer Lewis's writings as translated and spoken by Raymond Bernard (1923–2006), a writer and esotericist who was Grand Master of several western initiatory traditions. Bernard travelled widely to create spiritual and fraternal links between different communities and religious and spiritual organisations including ancient Egyptian traditions, Buddhism, Hinduism, and Sikhism. In addition to the spoken words using invocation and instruction, there are occasional loud bursts of Hindu-style chanting (Aum, Ra etc.). It is designed as a 'particular experience' of the diverse and mystical work of the Rosicrucian world, a lecture in the occult with practical applications (breathing exercises) for which the listener is bid to 'sit down', observe and engage, as in any religious ceremony. Lewis

drew the illustration on the cover of the LP: a dramatic Gothic church most closely resembling the cathedral at Chartres (famous for its 'rose' stained glass window) but probably a generic imagination of the symbol of spirituality.

Disque Rosicrucien is a recording of an esoteric ritual, using the power of recorded sound and the medium of the vinyl LP to enact an occult ceremony. The Rosicrucian project was designed to reveal hitherto unknown and hidden knowledge and this recording is designed in its own small way to aid in the acquisition of such enlightenment.

A. K. Salim · Afro-Soul / Drum Orgy

PRESTIGE

< A F R O - S O U L / D R U M O R G Y >

AFRO-SOUL / DRUM ORGY
A.K. SALIM (PRESTIGE, 1965)

The percussive dimension of ritual was not lost on experimental jazz musicians of the 1960s seeking to expand the dimensions of musical expression. It was at this point in the emergence of modern jazz that the origins of black music were explicitly and deliberately foregrounded. The increasing awareness and exploration of African tribal rhythms within African American communities represented an investment in the cultural heritage of former enslaved communities, leading to the development of a vast range of new forms of jazz and soul music.

Ahamd Khatab Salim was an American band leader who before *Afro-Soul / Drum Orgy* had been a Bebop arranger. The LP can be seen as an attempt at highlighting the African drum in

Tracks

> AFRIKA (AFRICA)
> NGOMBA YA TEMPO (ELEPHANT DANCE)
> KUMUAMKIA MZULU (SALUTE TO A ZULU)
> PEPO ZA SARARI (TRADE WINDS)

a western musical context as a sacred object, the 'tangible form of a divinity'.[41] While there are other instruments prominent on the LP (trumpet, saxophone, flute), it is the drum that lies at the heart of *Afro-Soul / Drum Orgy*, as if acknowledging the centrality of the instrument in the intense and often lengthy ceremonies of African cultures.

According to Salim, the musical elements of the recording all stemmed initially from the drum patterns; it was the 'African' dimension

---

41 Alfred Metraux, *Voodoo*, p.182.

Afro-Soul / Drum Orgy

PRESTIGE 7379

PRESTIGE

A. K. SALIM, conductor, composer, arranger
JOHN COLES, trumpet
PAT PATRICK, baritone sax, alto sax, flute
YUSEF ABDUL LATEEF, tenor sax, flute, argol
PHILEMON HOU, African xylophone, tambor drum
OSVALDO MARTINEZ, bongo, cowbell, conga
JULIO CALLAZO, shakers, conga
MARCELINO VALDES, conga
JUAN CADAVIEJO, conga
WILLIAM CORREA, timbales

Side A
1. AFRIKA (AFRICA) 9:40
2. NGOMBA YA TEMPO (ELEPHANT DANCE) 9:40

Side B
1. KUMUAMKIA MZULU (SALUTE TO A ZULU) 7:00
2. PEPO ZA SARARI (TRADE WINDS) 8:00

According to Leonard Feather, Ahmad Khatab Salim was, during the middle and late 1950s, "one of the more important Bop-derived big-band arrangers on the New York scene." This album, the first of his own in some time, represents a radical departure for Salim—most of whose music since the 50s had continued to be directly informed by the Bop period.

Salim was born in Chicago on July 28, 1922 and majored in music while at DuSable high school where Bennie Green, Gene Ammons and Dorothy Donegan were also in attendance. Originally he was a reed player (clarinet and alto saxophone) as well as a composer, arranger and conductor and, beginning in 1939, he worked in the former capacity with a number of midwestern bands including Tiny Bradshaw's (the "Jersey Bounce" band—Salim played second alto and took most of the solos) and King Kolax' (an aggregation in which Salim's former schoolmates, Green and Ammons, also held chairs). He also played with groups led by Milt Buckner and Clark Terry, among others, and, after coming to New York, was in frequent presence at Minton's at the inception of the Bop movement and a close associate of that revolution's greatest hero, Charlie Parker, as well as Lester Young, Thelonious Monk and Dizzy Gillespie. A dislocated jaw, suffered in 1944, forced Salim to halt his career as an instrumentalist and it was left for him to devote all of his energies to writing. In addition to working and recording extensively as a leader, Salim has supplied charts for many bands of the past and present, notably those of Lucky Millinder (for whom he was a staff arranger), Count Basie, Woody Herman, Cab Calloway, Jimmy Lunceford, Billy Eckstine, Tito Puente, Dizzy Gillespie, Machito and Lionel Hampton. **Blee Blop Blues** (originally **Normania**), a standard in the Basie book, is probably Salim's best known composition.

In 1948, when many bands broke up because of the recording ban, Salim began, of economic necessity, to engage himself in diverse extra-musical activities (photography is a special passion—he also studied documentary film making) to which he intermittently subordinated his music. But music remained his central commitment and with recent years, and intensive studies at the Manhattan School of Music ("to broaden my technique and scope in the light of all the new developments in music") it has become, once again, his preoccupation. He would like, someday, to compose the music for his own films.

Among the arrangers and composers whom Salim favors and counts as his principal sources of inspiration are the late Tadd Dameron, Neal Hefti, Gil Evans, Melba Liston and Gerald Wilson.

As I said earlier, this recording departs from what Salim's previous work has been about. The idea for it came from A&R man Ozzie Cadena. It was his conception to build the framework of the album out of African rhythms and for the music to be completely spontaneous—no charts were used, and there were no rehearsals. All that was predetermined was the African context.

"The musicians came to the date cold," Salim says. "All the composing was done right on the date—we just talked over what we were going to do and did it—and with the exception of **Salute To A Zulu** which required two takes, all the numbers were completed on the first take. The basic inspiration for the horns was drawn from whatever the drums were doing. Willie Bobo's assistance in getting us the drummers was most invaluable. For the most part I just told the drummers to get it started. Julio Callazo knew some African rhythms and helped to set patterns for the drummers. The horns were playing for **sounds** rather than traditional or conventional jazz lines—their impressions of how Africa sounds, inspired by the drums. They were really having a conversation, not just playing in a traditional jazz way."

Excepting Philemon Hou, a Zulu who was working at the World's Fair at the time (**Salute To A Zulu** was built "around a little thing Philemon was doing on the African xylophone—a small xylophone supported by the lap), all of the percussionists are Latins who have had experience in Afro-Cuban music. On **Africa, Elephant Dance, Salute To A Zulu** and **Trade Winds** they create varying and interesting rhythmic patterns and succeed in generating a considerable heat over which the three exceptional horn players, Pat Patrick, Yusef Lateef and John Coles give their "impressions of the sounds of Africa" with fire and abandon. The method and manner result in some exciting and intriguing music.

Salim feels that this recording has "inspired and opened up a new outlook" for him. "This date was still bound to a formal concept, though it moved toward something that is more 'free.' I'd like to combine this kind of concept with the more formalized kind of writing in the future. This recording was so much fun to make."

Notes: Robert Levin (April 1965)
Supervision: Ozzie Cadena
Recording: Rudy Van Gelder

For free catalog send to **PRESTIGE RECORDS INC.,** 203 SO. WASHINGTON AVE., BERGENFIELD, N.J.

BACK

< A F R O - S O U L / D R U M O R G Y >

of the rhythm that determined the improvised form. The musicians on this record are, apart from a tambor/marimba player called Philemon Hou (a 'Zulu', according to the sleeve notes), of Afro-Cuban descent, with horn players (including Yusef Lateef and the more obscure but excellent Pat Patrick) rendering what Salim admits are an 'impression of the sounds of Africa'. The titles of the cuts on the LP convey this vaguely touristic sonic imagining of the continent.

'Afrika' launches us straight into the wild fusion of elements at hand here, a frantic 10-minute epic of African percussion — mainly drums and bells — mixed with vaguely dissonant free jazz elements. As the track progresses the traditional jazz instruments gradually match the frenzy of the drums and percussion before bowing out in an apparent admission of defeat. 'Ngomba Ya Tempo' is much slower and gentler but no less relentless in terms of the hypnotic percussive rhythms, an African xylophone gradually emerging out of the pulse and claiming some space. Engineer Rudy Van Gelder occasionally embellishes the sound with subtle reverb effects. 'African' chants in a mimesis of ritual choral incantations appear just as the track is closing. On 'Kumuamkia Mzulu' the xylophone becomes a solo instrument. The repetition of the track and the gradual introduction of the piercing 'argol' (arghul) pipe induces a trance-like mood. 'Pepo Za Sarari' is again relentless, but the insistent conga and timbale beat creates an irresistible and powerful contemporary groove rising to a sudden and dramatic ending.

Overall, the LP does a good job of impersonating the orgiastic dimension to certain instances of African ritual. The stripped-down minimalism of the LP means it holds up well today and it must have been, or will be, widely sampled by new generations of sound designers. Some critics have likened the recording to an instance of 'blaxploitation' where western musicians have crudely translated indigenous cultures for commercial gain. The rich and complex traditions of African and Afro-Cuban drumming (for example, Batá) are reduced to

< R I T U A L >

simplistic mimicry and the sacred use of the African percussion ignored or abstracted. Afro-Cuban jazz has certainly played on the erotic connotations of the percussion pulse, adopting, as John Corbett points out, a set of 'mildly offensive stereotypes' to sell records.[42]

On the other hand, one could read *Afro-Soul / Drum Orgy* as an interesting experiment in fusing the ancient and the modern, the jazz musicians of the twentieth century paying homage to their ancestors from whom so much was taken. Despite reservations about the 'Zulu' stock footage on the cover, suggesting some ethnographic authenticity, *Afro-Soul / Drum Orgy* is a fascinating western utilisation of the power of unfiltered African rhythms to create a fresh musical form. Salim claimed the experience of making the recording 'opened a new outlook' for him, an expansion of

consciousness through a new form of musical ritual. As Corbett suggests in *Vinyl Freak*, this is nothing less than what John Coltrane did with *Africa/Brass* or what Sun Ra was doing with his Afro-Futurism project, but to ultimately much wider acclaim.

---

42 John Corbett, *Vinyl Freak*, p.48. 'Philomen Huo' is rumoured in some quarters to be none other than legendary South African trumpet player Hugh Masakela, although why Masakela would be reduced to percussion duties is unexplained.

< A BLACK MASS >

A BLACK MASS
LEROI JONES (JIHAD PRODUCTIONS, 1968)

'THE BLACK ARTIST'S ROLE IN AMERICA IS TO AID IN THE DESTRUCTION OF AMERICA AS HE KNOWS IT'. (AMIRI BARAKA, 'STATE/MEANT')

Tracks

> A BLACK MASS
> A BLACK MASS

As a radical (and controversial) playwright and poet LeRoi Jones (born Everett Leroy Jones and subsequently known as Amira Baraka) sought to completely subvert repressive and neo-colonial ideologies and practices. Baraka sought to take control of the word/concept 'black' and use it in a variety of radical new ways. His books, including poetry collection *Black Magic* (1969), *Black Fire* (1968), a collection of essays by prominent black writers and thinkers, and *Black Music* (1968), a study of African American sound forms, all make new use of the word. At the same time music played a critical part in Barak's creativity, thinking, and living.

His construction/reinvention of a 'Black Mass' was designed to look at symbols of black African oppression from an entirely new and radical perspective. The 'Black Mass' is not an outdated ancient primitive ritual but can be re-imagined as a modern invocation of power and freedom.

Baraka's experience of institutional racism, initially while as a gunner in the US Air Force, fueled his subsequent radical stance and it

a black mass

by Amiri Baraka (LeRoi Jones)
Sun Ra and the Myth Science Arkestra

< A B L A C K M A S S >

was through 'beat' and avant-garde poetry and jazz music that he persistently expressed his political consciousness. New forms of poetry and writing were to mix with new forms of music and sound to create a radical form of collective free spirituality (found in the black avant-garde of John Coltrane, Albert Ayler, Sun Ra, etc.), 'an emotionalism that seeks freedom',[43] a 'Unity Music'[44] that brought together jazz, blues, and religious and secular forms of expression.

A Black Mass is a play (credited to 'Imamu Baraka') but is of interest here in a book about music as the accompaniment for the production was provided by The Sun Ra Arkestra. The play was written in 1965 (according to Jones this was at his desk at the Black Arts Repertory Theater School [BARTS] in New York), but the recording took place at another theatre, The Spirit House. The text is an 'origin myth' that betrays the influence of the Nation of Islam which Baraka was to split from soon after. Staying true to the radical doctrines of Black Power, Baraka inverts the idea (and the common idea of the 'Black Mass') that white symbolizes good and black symbolizes evil. Here, the actors' words express the idea that beauty is associated with 'blackness'.

Sun Ra was a prominent supporter of BARTS, teaching musical composition and anything else that people would engage with. The entire production of A Black Mass is avant-garde in form: actors speak improvised chaotic pseudo-philosophical 'Myth-Science' phrases designed to be what Baraka called "other-worldly". Disrupted by the creation of a 'white beast', black characters shout and scream the words in a confrontational manner. The idea of Afro-Futurism plays a strong part in the sound of the production. The desire is to express new forms of 'science', 'history', and 'human development' through a radical black consciousness. Brechtian 'alienation' dramatic techniques are expanded into a futuristic science fiction dimension. At the same time,

---

43 Amiri Baraka, Black Music.
44 Leroi Jones, 'The Changing Same' in The Leroi Jones/ Amiri Baraka Reader, p.209.

< RITUAL >

restrictive white European concepts must be challenged and negated as part of the 'denying or withholding of all signposts'.[45] Baraka's text foregrounds the idea that, like the blues singers before them, African American writers and poets had to adapt and reinterpret the world that white oppression had dealt them. *A Black Mass* ends with the words "Al-Ism al-A'zam" ("May God have mercy") repeated continuously until the lights go out.

In terms of music, *A Black Mass* begins with a cacophony of noise that settles down into a form of rhythmic chanting. The Arkestra's interventions range from smatterings of drum kit rolls and electric organ doodling to an entire theme that weaves in and out, 'The Satellites Are Spinning', later appearing on Sun Ra's 1972 BYG LP *The Solar-Myth Approach Vol. 1*. The 'out there' dimension to all of Sun Ra's music appealed to Baraka as an expression of a new cosmic dimension ('Science-Fact',

he called it), as it has done to many fans and admirers throughout the maestro's long and strange career.

It is possible to see *A Black Mass* as a pioneering work in the radical arts, exploring the 'possibility of expanding what can be recorded and what kind of collaborations between word and music'[46] can be achieved The idea of the 'Mass' is updated and rendered using modern music and dance into a contemporary context within a particular social and cultural epoch; not as something 'backward' and 'superstitious', but as way of resetting the way we think about race, gender, and freedom.

Note: Initial vinyl copies of *A Black Mass* were limited, and numerous bootleg versions of the recording have since circulated, including the one used for this review.

45 John Hentoff and McCarthy quoted in *Amir Baraka, Blues People*, p.32.
46 Amiri Baraka, *A Black Mass*, sleeve notes.

< L A P S Y C H O S O M N I E M E T H O D E C O N T R E L ' I N S O M N I E >

LA PSYCHOSOMNIE
METHODE CONTRE L'INSOMNIE
DOMINIQUE WEBB (MAGIC DISC, 1970)

Tracks

> LA PSYCHOSOMNIE (RELAXATION)
> MÉTHODE CONTRE L'INSOMNIE

The various video clips circulating on the internet of French hypnotist Dominique Webb show a flamboyantly dressed long-haired individual trawling the streets for victims of his occult art. There is something comical about the way that Webb suddenly launches into his wide-eyed stare, homing in on innocent bystanders (often young women) on a café terrace to entrance with his magic powers and piercing blue eyes. He accosts young girls in parks, mesmerizing them with his magic card and rope tricks. He sends girls into a trance and weaves his hands over their prostrate bodies. He appears in a formal classroom setting teaching youngsters the various arts of illusionism. A surreal sequence shows Webb hypnotizing a row of seated figures in a Parisian street, supposedly having convinced them that they have taken a large dose of LSD. Webb is also seen roaring around in a sports car driving blindfolded while wearing a black hood, an action for which, despite his claims that he possessed 'in-built radar', he was occasionally arrested. Other clips show him piercing people's cheeks with large needles and making a man lie down on a broken light bulb while a motorcycle rides over his chest. All this develops the definite impression that Webb has created an image as the 'rock star of psychic phenomenon'.

DOMINIQUE WEBB LA PSYCHOSOMNIE
METHODE CONTRE L'INSOMNIE

< L A   P S Y C H O S O M N I E   M E T H O D E   C O N T R E   L ' I N S O M N I E   >

This Johnny Hallyday of ESP and illusionism was media-savvy and made frequent cameos on television and newsreels during the late 1960s and 1970s, including pop music shows with celebrities such as Claude François, Annie Philippe, and Dalida, and was also the star of The Witchcraft Festival at The Olympia in Paris in 1969. Webb became a celebrity combining showmanship with a hint of the occult at precisely the time such fascinations with art and the supernatural merged. However, it is worth noting that hypnotism has been popular in France for some time before, from the pioneering work of 18th-century monk Abbé Faria who was the first to define the practice as operating purely by the power of suggestion, to the infamous experiments carried out by psychologist Jean-Martin Charcot using hypnosis on 'hysterical' women patients in the Salpêtrière Hospital, to the work of Émile Coué in the twentieth century who had a method of hypnotism named after him. Webb was a continuation of this tradition in the 'space-age', producing books, opening

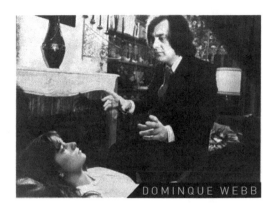

DOMINQUE WEBB

a magic shop in Paris, and releasing this LP recording of hypnotism in action.

La Psychosomnie is an LP devoted to using sound to explain the art of parapsychic phenomena. Initial copies of the LP came supplied with several inserts designed to aid in the hypnotism of the listener (these elements rarely survive today), including a sheet of patterned paper designed to be rolled and then placed on top of the swirling label while the disc rotates; a small silver card to be placed on top of the cone, and a blank sheet of paper to protect the cone. Some video clips of Webb

PARIS MATCH — Au Moyen-Age, WEBB aurait été brûlé. On laisse entendre que les médecins viendraient le consulter maintenant officiellement... Passant parmi les spectateurs, Dominique WEBB, les yeux bleus fixes, le masque figé, les voir instantané, les endort tous très vite.

TELE 7 JOURS — (Geneviève Coste) — 2.5.8. — En dix minutes, ces trois chiffres avaient fait de lui un homme célèbre, car c'étaient des chiffres magiques, ceux du tiercé du prix de Diane. A Télé-Dimanche, Dominique WEBB avait donné le résultat de ce tiercé un quart d'heure avant l'arrivée de la course. L'affaire avait fait grand bruit.

Quatre mois plus tard, il renouvelait à bord du France son exploit de la télévision. L'intérêt qu'il porte à l'hypnose remonte d'ailleurs à son enfance. « Déjà à l'école, je m'étais rendu compte de mon pouvoir, raconte-t-il. J'étais un cancre, et quand un professeur voulait m'interroger, je m'amusais à le regarder fixement. Mon regard le détournait sur un autre élève, ou le forçais à m'interroger le jour où, par hasard, j'avais appris ma leçon. Plus tard j'ai continué à m'exercer pendant une heure chaque jour. Cela donne des résultats. J'ai réussi parfois à influencer les clients de ma fabrique : je suis parvenu à faire parler normalement un bègue. Et je m'hypnotise moi-même grâce à un jeu de miroirs.

L'EXPRESS — (Claude Veillot) — On verra placardé à l'Opéra Dominique WEBB endormir des passants volontaires, qui seront ensuite exposés, momies vivantes, dans la vitrine d'un grand magasin.

« Par auto-suggestion, je viens de me faire maigrir de quinze kilos en un mois ». En France Dominique WEBB est le seul à présenter sur scène un spectacle d'hypnose. Il ne joue pas pour autant les apprentis sorciers : « Je ne fais pas de miracles, dit-il, mon pourcentage de réussite varie entre 60 et 70 %.

PARIS JOUR — « J'AI BIEN DORMI A L'OLYMPIA » — Avant toute chose, je dois préciser que cet article pourra paraître étrange à certains. Ce n'est pas ma faute. C'est celle de l'hypnotiseur Dominique WEBB. J'ai eu l'imprudence de monter

sur la scène de l'Olympia avec une douzaine d'autres personnes, pour lui servir de cobaye. Il nous a endormis. Pendant notre sommeil, il paraît que nous nous sommes livrés à des actes étranges, comme danser la PATCHANGA, rire aux éclats au spectacle imaginaire d'un film comique, ou nous déshabiller, nous croyant dans le désert.

FRANCE SOIR (Thérèse Fournier) — « A 12 ans, j'ai commencé à m'apercevoir de mes capacités hypnotiques, dit-il. » si bien qu'à 15 ans, Dominique WEBB né WEBER, dans l'Aude, dans une famille d'industriels, a commencé un numéro d'hypnotisme... à 27 ans, il est devenu à la fois homme d'affaires (il possède une fabrique de jouets et de prestidigitation) et il a créé une école.

L'AURORE (Dominique MISLER) — A 27 ans, WEBB, des yeux innocemment bleu (c'est pour mieux vous tromper mon enfant), est en effet le (jeune) roi de l'hypnose. L'homme capable d'endormir, s'il l'envie soudain l'en prend, toute une salle de spectateurs, en moins d'un quart d'heure... Pour WEBB « l'hypnose c'est l'art de conditionner une personne, de tenir en domination son esprit suffisamment pour lui faire accepter des choses qui ne sont pas. Ainsi je peux parfaitement persuader un sujet « en état » qu'il se trouve en plein Sahara sous un soleil de plomb. Les incrédules le verront transpirer à grosses gouttes, enlever sa veste, sa chemise au besoin ».

ICI PARIS — Déjà, au siècle dernier, Charco avait étudié les phénomènes dits paranormaux. Il avait constaté que l'hypnose, c'est-à-dire la mise en sommeil artificiel d'un sujet, est réalisable sous certaines conditions. Depuis ce temps là, des opérations chirurgicales sous hypnose ont été réalisées aux Etats-Unis et quelques unes en France. La mise en condition hypnotique d'un sujet n'est pas une affaire de fluide, comme on le croit souvent. Il suffit d'avoir une volonté plus forte que celle de son sujet et de lui imposer cette volonté. Le sujet doit être d'accord pour s'endormir. S'il cherche à résister, il n'y a que peu de chances de réussir. Il faut accepter l'hypnose comme une sorte de somnifère.

METHODE

Elle ne présente aucun danger. Vous allez-vous « assoupir » par « suggestion », mais votre sommeil sera tout à fait naturel. Le réveil se fera également très normalement, quand vous serez suffisamment reposés auprès à la sonnerie de votre réveil. La méthode est très simple. Si vous souhaitez simplement vous relaxer, vous écoutez la face A du disque. Si vous souhaitez vous endormir, vous écoutez la face B. Vous devez être confortablement installés, sur un lit ou dans un fauteuil. Vous écoutez attentivement et vous ne pensez à rien d'autre. Vous êtes dans l'obscurité totale, à l'exception d'une seule source de lumière, celle d'une bougie (si quelqu'un reste près de vous) ou d'une lampe torche, glacée entre l'électrophone et vous. Dans le cas de la lampe électrique, son faisceau lumineux sera dirigé sur le « tube magnétique ». Le « tube magnétique » est un objet hypnotique.

Vous le confectionnerez en roulant en tube (collée ou agrafée) la feuille spéciale que vous trouverez dans l'album de disque. Ce « tube magnétique » surmonté de la plaquette métallisée (comme indiqué sur le « roули ») sera placé au centre du disque. Vous devez sans cesse conserver votre regard sur cet objet. Vous pouvez remplacer la « fixation intensive » du tube par celle de la spirale servant d'étiquette au disque lui-même.

Vous ne vous endormirez peut être pas dès la première audition du disque. Ne vous décourager pas. Écoutez le plusieurs fois de suite jusqu'à ce que sommeil s'ensuive. Lorsque vous vous serez endormis une fois par cette méthode, il est très probable que, par la suite, vous sombrerez dans le plus profond des sommeils après seulement quelques minutes d'audition, grâce à un réflexe mécanique.

STEREO-MONO

DILLARD et Cie, Imp, Paris   Imprimé en France

INSIDE RIGHT

**DOMINIQUE
WEBB
LA PSYCHOSOMNIE
METHODE CONTRE
L'INSOMNIE**

BACK

< L A   P S Y C H O S O M N I E   M E T H O D E   C O N T R E   L ' I N S O M N I E   >

are book-ended by the swirling vortex graphic that is central to hypnotic practice and that appears as a label design on this LP.

La Psychosomnie is certainly a mesmerizing experience. The music and effects accompanying Webb's evocative voice instructing the listener on how to combat insomnia (effects which are, according to the LP credits, created by him), comprise spacey blobs of electronic sound laid over eerie and constantly shifting chord progressions. Webb's voice is laden with audio effects such as echo and reverb, emphasizing the method of dream-state hypnotism. Side one is devoted to relaxing the listener, creating a preparatory state of calm and receptiveness to being hypnotised. Side two opens with a more rhythmic electronic rhythm akin to a supernatural soundtrack score. This pulses all the way through the side, creating a magical and entrancing effect. The somewhat disturbing LP cover features Webb's staring eyes while the back cover includes his full face, making commercial use of Webb's most notable and arresting asset.

Webb also later released *Hypnose* on Les Disques Motors, a 'hypnotism' single with music by Jean-Michel Jarre. *Hypnose* was a much more commercial-sounding work featuring drums, synth riffs, and the kinds of pop arrangements that Jarre would soon become famous for with his smash LP *Oxygène* (recorded for the same label). The cover featured an extreme close-up of an eye staring out from between bloody horror film style lettering.

< R I T U A L >

Webb's strange legacy continued in 2007 when French sound artist Vincent Epplay released a recording based on Webb's antics made as a contribution to the sound installation Station des Ondes, part of the La Traversée festival that took place on 29–30 December 2007. This was a cultural project that transformed the old municipal funeral services building in Paris into a multi-disciplinary modern art space. Epplay's interpretation of the Webb record, with added samples from films and other media, is far woozier and more disconcerting, emphasizing the general weirdness of the original record and suggesting hypnotism is a key aspect of modern mysticism.

Dominique Webb defined his work as 'the art of deceiving others to entertain them' and *La Psychosomnie* made a notable contribution to this. He died in 2019; thirteen years earlier he had been involved in a terrible skiing accident from which he never properly recovered.

< LE TRADIZIONI MUSICALI IN PUGLIA >

LE TRADIZIONI MUSICALI IN PUGLIA VOL. 3 — MUSICHE E BALLI TRADIZIONALI DEL SALENTO — PIZZICA TARANTA

VARIOUS, COMPILED BY GIUSEPPE MICHELE GALA (TARANTA, 2003)

Tracks

> PIZZICA TARANTATA INDIAVOLATA
> PIZZICA TARANTATA SORDA
> PIZZICA PIZZICA DI CORIGLIANO
> PIZZICA PIZZICA DI NOCIGLIA
> PIZZICA SCHERMA A TORREPADULI
> PIZZICA PIZZICA DI CUTROFIANO
> PIZZICA PIZZICA DI MARTANO
> SCOTIS DI CUTROFIANO
> SCOTIS DI CORIGLIANO
> POLKA DI NOCIGLIA
> QUADRIGLIA
> QUADRIGLIE E TARANTELLE
> TARANTELLA
> VALZERE A STRISCIO
> MARZUCCA DI CORIGLIANO
> VALZER DI GIOVANNINO (CHIRIATTI)

Tracks cont.

> POLKA DI CHIRIATTI
> SCOTIS DI CARPIGNANO
> QUADRIGLIA (A CORIGLIANO)
> QUADRIGLIA (A NOCIGLIA)
> PIZZICA PIZZICA
> LA 'NZEGNA (PIZZICA PIZZICA)
> PIZZICA PIZZICA DI CELLINO
> PIZZICA PIZZICA A SANTU PAULU
> CANTO DI UNA TARANTATA

In 2006 and 2008, I embarked on a series of pilgrimages, not in search of tarantism, but the pizzica tarantella, the music that cured the *taranti*. *Tarantati*, or tarantism, is the term given to a form of hysteria observed in

PIZZICA TARANTA

Musiche e balli tradizionali del Salento

suoni e balli in Italia · musique et danse d'Italie   ETHNICA   musica y baile en Italia · music and dance of Italy

23

Le tradizioni musicali in Puglia - Vol. 3

a cura di Giuseppe Michele Gala

Introduzione di Eugenio Imbriani

< LE TRADIZIONI MUSICALI IN PUGLIA >

Southern Italy. The bite of the tarantula spider is said to inspire convulsions that might last for days or weeks and can only be cured by music: the *tarantella*, a repetitive melody over an incessant beat performed chiefly on violins, accordions, and tambourines.

One early documented case encapsulates the otherworldly dynamic. A letter published in the September 1753 edition of *The Gentleman's Magazine* recalls a strange scene outside Naples. The author of the letter, a visiting English music student by the name of Stephen Storace, witnesses a man lying prone on the street and is implored by the gathered crowd to play the tarantella on the violin he carries. He doesn't know the tune but when the melody is sung to him ('a kind of jig') he quickly learns it and the man on the ground becomes animated with the first bars, 'as if he had been awaken'd by some frightful vision, and wildly star'd about still moving every joint of his body'. When the musician stops playing, the man falls back down as if suffering 'miserable agonies'. The frightened Storace:

MONTEFALCIONE 2008

'made all the haste I could to learn the rest of the tune; which done, I play'd near him, I mean about four yards from him, the instant he heard me, he rose up as he did before, and danced as hard as any man could do; his dancing was very wild, he kept a perfect time in the dance, but had neither, rules, nor manners, only jumped, and runned, too and from, made very comical postures [...] and otherwise every thing was very wild of what he did [...] and then the people cried out — faster — faster: meaning that I should give a quicker motion to the tune, which I did, so quick, that I

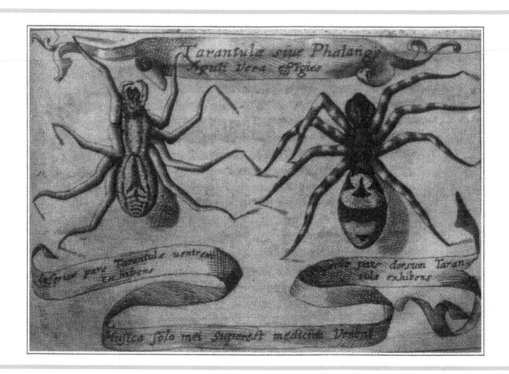

TA023 - 2003

< LE TRADIZIONI MUSICALI IN PUGLIA >

could hardly keep up playing, and the man still danced in time.'[47]

The student plays for around two hours without interval as the crowd mops the sweat from his brow and fan him to keep cool. The lore has not changed since the letter was published: the bite of the tarantula, taking place when the victim is working or napping in a field, induces a condition that, if untreated, may result in death. Fortunately, fatalities are uncommon because, as Storace says, a priest is often on hand with a violin to provide a 'cure'.

In 1959, the anthropologist Ernesto De Martino took an interdisciplinary team to the Salentine Peninsula of Puglia, Southern Italy, to investigate the phenomenon that had existed in the area for centuries. He concluded that tarantism is influenced by a variety of cultural and interpersonal factors, steeped in folklore, and not a mental illness.

---

47 Stephen Storace, 'Of the Tarantula, by an Italian Gentleman,' *The Gentleman's Magazine* XXIII (London, Sept. 1753), pp.433–434.

My own journey was to towns and villages, beginning in Campania where Stephen Storace, our Victorian music student, also 'began', representing for me both a literal and metaphysical embarkation point. On feast days musicians parade through the streets. In Montemarano, these musicians are unlike others, bedecked in robes and masks. I also encountered the Montemarano musicians on the cobbled streets of nearby Montefalcione, another mountain village, and followed them between groups of other itinerant musicians, the noise overlapping in strange, hypnotic unity on our way to the Mother Church.

The landscape changes dramatically on leaving Campania. Headed for Puglia, the 'heel' of Italy, the mountains and lush vegetation become arid and flat. Parts of it have the air of a dilapidated gas station, in constant retreat from the blazing sun. My destination now was Galatina, the village where De Martino conducted his field studies. Otranto is a coastal town some twenty miles east of Galatina. It was here that my troublesome rented automatic

CHAPEL OF ST PAUL

refused to start and a bunch of passing lads stopped to help, doing so with such gusto that it seemed to me this was the reason they had got up in the morning. Yet, one person in the group, older than the rest, did nothing but stand watching with his arms folded. No one in the group acknowledged him, they were all preoccupied in any case, but soon I was feeling drained by the impassive presence and the steadfast gaze. Only later did I realise the man had placed the Evil Eye on me, a curse. Whether one believes in the superstition and lore of the south, or anywhere else for that matter, the sensation I felt following the

encounter was real; the ability to acknowledge and respond to it broke its power and this put me in mind of the *taranti*.

Galatina sits in the middle of the Salento area, between Otranto and Gallipoli, and the Ionian and Adriatic seas. The Romanesque Church of Saint Catherine of Alexandria and the piazza with its baroque façades are the ancient backdrop to the feast day of Saints Peter and Paul. I arrived at midday, the streets empty except for a drunk man who warned me to be careful. I visited the chapel of St Paul, the locus of tarantism, documented by De Martino and from where the most arresting images of tarantism originate.

Around the corner from the chapel is a temporary exhibition devoted to tarantism, which contains many archive photos of *taranti*, peasants seemingly possessed, and new artwork, acknowledging an edgier side to the celebrations. It is while perusing the exhibition, located in a room that overlooks the square, that the first soundcheck takes place. On the

< LE TRADIZIONI MUSICALI IN PUGLIA >

PIZZICA TARANTA MARIA DI NARDO

stage erected in the piazza, musicians play the *pizzicarella*, amplified to concert level, which brings the unnerving and violent images momentarily to life.

Later, the square is filled with people and night falls black against the illuminations, hundreds of lightbulbs forming archways across the piazza. Many people dance to the

< R I T U A L >

music, in groups and in pairs, but I spy a space in which an old man dances alone. But 'dance' is too simple a word for it. He has entered a catatonic state brought about by the music, removed himself from everything around him, distorting his face, thrusting his limbs edgily in all directions before stopping still for several seconds and then launching himself again. He appears dressed for the farm. To other dancers the old man is an alien, out of touch. While all around is joy, he is distant, the figure in the eighteenth-century monograph, the subject of the letter from the musician visitor, for whom music somehow serves to realign the brain, causing reality to explode back into focus.

Away from the concert stage are musicians who begin to play for their own entertainment. At 4:30 the following morning, when everything else has long since ended, these musicians are still playing. They form two camps. The musicians come and go; when one tires or gives up, another takes their place, and frequently swap from one group to the other. The melodies are the pizzica tarantella, driven by pounding tambourines of nine or ten or more. By my calculation this beat commenced at around 10pm and remained constant.

✦ ✦ ✦

There are many albums devoted to the music of the Italian south, and many that contain the pizzica tarantata, the music that cures the *taranti*. *Le Tradizioni Musicali In Puglia Vol. 3* features field recordings from the Salento region, the focus of much of this article. It is part of the Ethnica series of CDs curated by Giuseppe Michele Gala, who, since 1979, has amassed recordings and documentation on traditional music and dance across Italy. Other CDs focus on other regions, each with an informative booklet. I picked up a bunch of them on my travels, but some are now available for sale online. The label behind the series, Taranta, is also a resource for Italian folk: taranta.it. DAVID KEREKES

< B I B L I O G R A P H Y >

REFERENCES

Cook, Richard and Morton, Brian. *The Penguin Guide to Jazz on CD* (Penguin, 2002)

Corbett, John. *Vinyl Freak: Letters to a Dying Medium* (Duke University Press, 2017)

Curti, Roberto. *Italian Gothic Horror Films, 1970–1979* (McFarland, 2017)

Deren, Maya. *The Voodoo Gods* (Paladin, 1975)

Deren, Maya. *Essential Deren* (Documentext, 2005)

Fox, Charles. *The Jazz Scene* (Hamlyn, 1972)

Frazer, James. *The Golden Bough* (Penguin Books, 1996)

Grasso, Stephen. 'Haunted Soundsystem', *Strange Attractor Journal*, 4 (Strange Attractor, 2011)

Girard, René. *Violence and the Sacred* (Bloomsbury, 2013)

Harris, William J. (ed.). *The LeRoi Jones/Amiri Baraka Reader* (Thunder's Mouth Press, 1991)

Larkin, Philip. *All What Jazz: A Record Diary* (Faber, 1985)

Metraux, Alfred. *Voodoo* (Sphere, 1974)

Michelet, Jules. *Satanism and Witchcraft* (Tandem, 1969)

Myers, Rollo H. *Erik Satie* (Dover, 1968)

Nicholls, Simon. *The Notebooks of Alexander Skryabin* (Oxford University Press, 2018)

O'Brien, Tim and Savage, Mike. *Naked Vinyl* (Chrysalis, 2002)

Rosenfeld, Gavriel David. *The Fourth Reich: The Specter of Nazism from World War II to the Present* (Cambridge University Press, 2019)

Scott, Cyril. *Music and Its Secret Influence: Throughout the Ages* (Aquarian Press, 1982)

Schieffelin, Edward L. 'Problematizing Performance', in Felicia Hughes-Freeland (ed.), *Ritual, Performance, Media* (Routledge, 1998), pp.194–207.

Taylor, Tot. *Voodoo: Hoochie Coochie and the Creative Spirit* (Riflemaker, 2009)

Turner, Victor W. 'Symbols in African Ritual', *Science*, 179 (16 Mar. 1973), pp.1100–05

Webb, Dominique. *L'hypnose et les phénomènes PSI* (Éditions Robert Laffont, 1976)

Yates, Frances A. *The Rosicrucian Enlightenment* (Routledge, 1972)

< R I T U A L >

ARTWORK & CREDITS

The Communazis Exposed By Their Own Words: Revolution Today In The U.S.A (unknown)

"A Genuine Tong Funeral" (Gary Burton) (Photos by Syes Fredens/J.M. Birraux)

Disque Rosicrucien (artwork by Dr H. Spencer Lewis)

Afro-Soul / Drum Orgy (A.K. Salim) (unknown)

Black Mass (Lucifer) (Jacket design by Virginia Clark)

White Mass/Black Mass (Alexander Scriabin) (Cover photograph by Ken Goldberg)

La Psychosomnie (Dominique Webb) (unknown)

A Black Mass (Amiri Baraka) (unknown)

Som (Persona) (Artwork: Mateus Mondini and Guilherme Chapado Gody. Photos: Campadello Family Archive)

Divine Horsemen: The Voodoo Gods of Haiti (Cover design by Teiji Ito)

Rites Of The Pagan (Elisabeth Waldo And Her Concert Orchestra) (unknown)

Riti, Magie Nere E Segrete Orge Nel Trecento... (Gianfranco Reverbi) (Graphic: Gianluca Alessandrini Studio. Cover design: Michele Targonato)

Ritual (Nico Gomez) (unknown)

< BIBLIOGRAPHY >

A word about this collection

"I PLAY BEST WHEN MY UNCONSCIOUS IS ALTERED" (JOHN FAHEY)

GATHERING OF THE TRIBE explores some of the most unusual and challenging recordings in the recent history of music that have in some way revealed divine and cosmic laws, voyaged to another world or have used sound as a tool for transformation. I have adopted the phrase 'heavy conscious creation' because the common affect of this kind of music is that it in some way profoundly re-orders the human organism. It is music that acts on the mind and body in a deep, spiritual, sometimes dangerous way.

GATHERING OF THE TRIBE is concerned with recorded music that contributes towards the shaping of: Cosmic Consciousness, Occult Traditions, Revolutions in Sound, Ancient Mysteries, Outsider Art and Mindfucking.

GATHERING OF THE TRIBE is not an attempt at defining any parameters of what is 'heavy consciousness' music. It is a personal selection dredged from years of seeking out and listening to obscure and difficult music; music that is profound but which was made for reasons which the creators and performer are often at pains to properly explain. William James wrote about the 'varieties of religious experience'. *Gathering of the Tribe* is a series about the varieties of occult musical experience.

GATHERING OF THE TRIBE

"This is not your average book of record art or writing."
Dave Thompson, *Goldmine*

The ongoing practical guide to the ultimate occult record collection.

Gathering of the Tribe Vol 1: Acid
80 pages / pbk 978-1-915316-03-5 / ebk 978-1-915316-04-2

Gathering of the Tribe Vol 2: Landscape
100 pages / pbk 978-1-909394-83-4 / ebk 978-1-909394-84-1

Gathering of the Tribe Vol 3: Ritual
90 pages / pbk 978-1-915316-21-9 / ebk 978-1-915316-22-6

Coming soon:

Gathering of the Tribe Vol 4: Sex

And the book before the series:

Gathering of the Tribe: Music and Heavy Conscious Creation
478 pages / pbk 9781900486859 / ebk 978-1-909394-07-0

Available from headpress.com

Printed in the USA
CPSIA information can be obtained
at www.ICGtesting.com
JSHW051934200923
48731JS00005B/26